Hollow

ALSO BY MYRNA B. SHURE

Raising a Thinking Child
(with Theresa Foy DiGeronimo)

Raising a Thinking Child Workbook
(with Theresa Foy DiGeronimo)

Raising a Thinking Preteen

Raising a Thinking Preteen

▲ ▲ ▲

The "I Can Problem Solve" Program for 8- to 12-Year-Olds

MYRNA B. SHURE, PH.D.,
with Roberta Israeloff

An Owl Book
Henry Holt and Company   New York

This book is dedicated to all the thinking preteens who will
help make this world a safe and compassionate place to live.

Henry Holt and Company, LLC
Publishers since 1866
115 West 18th Street
New York, New York 10011

Henry Holt® is a registered trademark
of Henry Holt and Company, LLC.

Published in Canada by Fitzhenry & Whiteside Ltd.,
195 Allstate Parkway, Markham, Ontario L3R 4T8.

Library of Congress Cataloging-in-Publication Data
Shure, Myrna B.
Raising a thinking preteen: the "I can problem solve" program
for 8- to 12-year-olds / Myrna B. Shure with Roberta Israeloff.
p.   cm.
Includes bibliographical references and index.
ISBN 0-8050-6642-X
1. Preteens—Psychology.   2. Interpersonal conflict in children.
3. Problem solving in children.   4. Social skills in children.
5. Child rearing.   I. Israeloff, Roberta, date.   II. Title.
BF723.I645S488   2000   99-36077
649'.125—dc21   CIP

Henry Holt books are available for special promotions and
premiums. For details contact: Director, Special Markets.

First published in hardcover in 2000
by Henry Holt and Company

First Owl Books Edition 2001

Printed in the United States of America

1   3   5   7   9   10   8   6   4   2

Contents

Acknowledgments

The roots of *Raising a Thinking Preteen* stem from my original research with George Spivack, my friend and mentor, with whom I worked for over twenty years. The foundation for this book was laid by our original research with preteens in schools, funded in part by the Prevention Research Branch, National Institute of Mental Health (Grant #s MH-27741 and MH-35989). After it became clear that parents in a wide variety of income levels could help their children as early as age three think for themselves in ways that could help them successfully solve everyday problems, and after being inspired by countless more parents of three- to seven-year-olds who tried the "I Can Problem Solve" approach (ICPS for short) described in my first book, *Raising a Thinking Child,* the idea to take the problem-solving approach to parents of children in the critically important preteen years was born. It began when Jillian Buchwald, a student of mine at MCP Hahnemann University, creatively adapted many of the lesson-games from the intermediate grade level school manual, *I Can Problem Solve,* for use with a child in that age group at home. That child, and soon many others, enjoyed the games and activities so much that I was encouraged to expand those ideas and create a full program for parents of preteens, and the result of those efforts is what is in this book.

Over the years, there have been many who have moved me to continue my work. In Illinois, a group of educators and other professionals formed an ICPS task force of Kane and DuPage Counties—now chaired by Sandra Baumgardner—who meet periodically to share ideas, information, and resources. Sandra, a community resource consultant at the DuPage County Health Department in Wheaton, Illinois, has enthusiastically informed me of the response to her work with traditional intact families, as well as of foster and blended families, and those who have been court-referred. That the problem-solving approach would be well received by children older than seven was evidenced by the many new ICPSers from the Mill Street School in Naperville, Illinois, where its principal, Ruth Cross, an ICPS trainer herself, has supported her social worker, Rebecca Smith-Andoh, to become a parent educator in that school. Others who began their ICPS work with teachers and parents of younger children and then extended it to the preteen years include Philinda Coleman, prevention coordinator of the Mental Health Association in Illinois, and appreciation is expressed to Jan Holcomb, its executive director, for her continued support; Dawn Oparah, educational consultant, Amadi Leadership Associates in Atlanta, Georgia; Kevin Hatcher, director of in-school programs, National Mental Health Association of Georgia, with the support of Cynthia Wainscott, executive director; Louise McGahran, an educational specialist in Philadelphia, Pennsylvania; and Gail Tunnick, formerly program coordinator, Mental Health Association in Collier County, Naples, Florida, and the support of her executive director, Dee Talty, is greatly appreciated.

Bonnie Aberson, a school psychologist in the Dade County, Florida, public schools, who worked with teachers and parents of younger children, has recently focused her efforts on children with special needs. I was heartened to learn that her doctoral dissertation, supported by Alfredo Ardilla, formerly professor at the Miami Institute of Psychology, showed that using strategies of ICPS with parents of eight-year-olds with Attention Deficit Hyperactivity Disorder (ADHD) led to dramatic changes in those children's behavior, and Bonnie now successfully applies ICPS for children with other special needs as well.

But ICPS as an approach to children's behavior could not become available to more families were it not for people in a position to make that possible. I want to thank Ann Wendel, president, and Russell Pence, director of marketing at Research Press, who first published my *I Can Problem Solve* (ICPS) programs for schools, on which my work with parents is based. I appreciate their continued support of extending ICPS for families, and for permission to include the Silly Skits in Chapter 4 and the "Did I ICPS Today" chart in Chapter 7. I also thank Anni Matsick for her expressive artwork in Chapters 3 and 5, and Anna Heilbrun, age 11, for creating the picture in Chapter 6.

It was Lynn Seligman, my agent, who believed in this book and made it possible, encouraged me to write it, and introduced me to Roberta Israeloff, without whom this book would never have come to life. Roberta calmed me down, helped me to think straight, and beautifully shaped the words and ideas in a way that people could read.

And once the manuscript was sent to Cynthia Vartan, my editor, she took charge and tuned it with fine points beyond what we would have thought possible. Cynthia nurtured this manuscript with the same brilliance and sensitivity that she did with *Raising a Thinking Child,* my first book for parents of three- to seven-year-olds. The joy of working with Cynthia was a significant factor that propelled me to venture into this new endeavor. And I want to extend a very special thank you to everyone at Henry Holt for their enthusiastic support of our completion of this book and for believing in how it can help families with children in their preteen years: John Sterling, president and publisher; Maggie Richards, vice-president and director of sales and marketing, Elizabeth Shreve, director of publicity, and Jennifer Barth, executive editor. I also want to thank Amelia Sheldon, editor, Jae Park and Marie Saraceni, assistant editors, and Rita Quintas, production editor, for their help and patience with me in putting together the finishing touches.

Most of all, I want to thank the kids and their parents who sparked so many of the ideas that went into the making of *Raising a Thinking Preteen*. One group of kids ages eight to twelve who were not part of my research, and whose thoughts or stories are in no way identified by name, deserve special recognition for the important insights they gave me about how kids think and feel about things: Farrah Ferguson, Kelli Ferguson, Anna Heilbrun, Alexia Houser, Kimberly Kane, Ben Katz, Elizabeth Katz, Matt Makransky, Maura Mullaney, Gabriela Laufman Kogut, Gaby Nolan, Kyle Nolan, Maxi Prinsen, Abby Shore, Scott Shore, and Bradley Zappala. These youngsters, and those who were a part of my research over the years, gave me new insights into my own thinking about what's really important in the world. I learned more from them than they could possibly have learned from me.

MBS

I'd like to thank Myrna Shure for the pleasure and ease of our collaboration, and for sharpening my own critical thinking skills; Cynthia Vartan for her clarifying eye; Lynn Seligman for her foresight and insight; and David, Ben, and Jake Fleisher, for standing by me and learning with me every step of the way.

RI

Preface

When I was writing my first book, *Raising a Thinking Child*, I wondered if parents of very young children, ages three to seven, would find the "I Can Problem Solve" (ICPS) method helpful, as I hoped it would be. The answer was a resounding "Yes!" Not only was the book a winner of a Parents' Choice Award in 1996, but many parents wrote to me and told me how delighted and astonished they were to see that their young children could learn to think ahead and solve problems on their own.

When children problem solve for themselves, their behavior changes in many positive ways, and parents who followed the ICPS method noted that their children's problematic behavior subsided. But they also noticed many other changes as well.

My son isn't so afraid of the other kids now. He's learned how to join them, not run away from them.

My daughter doesn't just think about herself anymore. She really seems to care now how others feel about things.

I didn't think ICPS was for me. I liked explaining why my son should do things. But we respect each other more now. He'd walk away while I was talking to him. He never heard a word I said. Now we listen to each other.

Perhaps most gratifying, parents discovered that they were changing along with their children.

Before ICPS I was hoping my child would learn to comply. Now I'm pleased she has learned to make good decisions by herself.

At first I was afraid to let him make his own decisions. Now I trust him more to make good ones.

It makes me think about what I'm doing.

I learned that I'm not the only one who has problems. I understand my child's problems better now too.

Now I see my child has feelings too, and he is more aware of mine.

I used to think I was protecting my child by making decisions for him. Now I see I am protecting him better by letting him make them himself.

As you can see, ICPS not only helps children think more clearly, but also enhances relationships, builds trust, and makes both parents and children more confident.

A child who learns to problem solve in her very early years will continue to do so. But it's also true that as children grow their decision-making capabilities are challenged in new ways. A preschooler who can ICPS her way out of an argument with a friend over a toy, for example, will need to learn more abstract skills as she grows in order to keep pace with the type of problems she will typically encounter, such as when a friend betrays her trust.

That's why I decided to write *Raising a Thinking Preteen*. In this book, I'll explain how older children, ages eight through twelve, can use ICPS skills to meet the array of situations they encounter at school, at home, and with their friends. It will expand on the skills presented in the first book, and add new skills that my research has shown can guide behavior beginning at age eight.

Fortunately, the ICPS method is eminently portable, and can be used in the elementary as well as the preschool years. In fact, ages eight to twelve are a special time, and offer families a unique opportunity. They are the years right before normal adolescent rebellion sets in, when parents may find it more difficult to talk things over.

Whether you are an experienced ICPS family, or using the method for the first time, *Raising a Thinking Preteen* will prove invaluable. It will help you answer the question "How can my child learn to solve the problems he's facing now, and in the future?"

It's never too late to become an ICPS family.

Raising a Thinking Preteen

Introduction

Ask parents of children between the ages of eight and twelve what they are most worried about, and you'll probably discover that they share many concerns:

> I want my daughter to have a good adjustment to middle school, and to make a commitment to not only stay in school but stay involved in school.

> I want my son to make good friends and stay away from the bad crowd.

> I want my daughter to refrain from using drugs and alcohol, and precocious sex, even if her friends are.

> I want my son to reject violence as a solution.

> I don't want my daughter to become a victim of violence.

Children have their own worries. Ask fifth graders what they're most concerned about when they consider the prospect of entering middle school or junior high, and most likely they'll say:

- "I'm worried about being picked on by bullies."
- "I want to be able to stand up for myself."
- "I don't want to be pressured into using drugs."

The common thread, as I read through this litany of hopes and fears, is clear. What parents want for their children—and children want for themselves—is to be able to make good decisions and to resolve conflict, whether the conflict is between peers, or with teachers or parents.

What helps children as they approach the preteen and teen years make good choices about their lives? Not slogans. They know that one-dimensional phrases like "Just say no" won't rescue them when they most need help. There is a real lifeline we can offer them: a set of specific skills that they can learn and master in order to become good problem solvers.

Here's a brief description of these skills:

Understanding another's feelings and point of view, which enables children to appreciate that everyone may not think and feel the same way about things;

Understanding motives, which enables children to understand that there may be reasons that propel people to do what they do *at a given moment*, and reasons beneath the surface that underlie behavior *over time*;

Finding alternative solutions, which encourages children to think of all of their options;

Considering consequences, which encourages children to think ahead;

Sequenced planning, which encourages children to make a sequenced plan that anticipates potential obstacles and considers timing issues, i.e., that problem solving takes time, and that some times are better than others for taking action.

Teaching these skills forms the cornerstone of *Raising a Thinking Preteen*. This book contains special activities and dialogues that you can use to respond to your child's problems in a new way—a way that will change your family dynamics and produce happy, self-confident, socially well-adjusted and emotionally intelligent children. And as Daniel Goleman so eloquently expressed in his book, *Emotional Intelligence*, children must be able to tune in to their own feelings and those of others before they can make good decisions at school, at home, on the playground, and in all their relationships.

No one wants their child to start fights, bully, or tease others. And no one wants their child to be the victim of those who act this way—not now, not later. Yet most of our children's conflicts are normal, even healthy. In fact, as Lynn Katz and her colleagues point out, they can be productive. Children eight to twelve are eminently capable of learning important lessons from disagreement: that their friends and acquaintances think and feel differently than they do about things, and as they grow, can come to better understand why people may do what they do. Once they've digested this vital information, they are ready to think about more options in terms of how they want to resolve these conflicts.

According to my research, which has been ongoing for the past twenty-five years, there's a crucial link between the ability to solve problems and emotional well-being. Here's an example of what I mean.

Ten-year-old Richard hit his younger brother, who was "bugging" him. When asked what happened next, Richard said, "He hit me back, but I don't care."

Ten-year-old Sam also hit his younger brother. When he was asked what happened next, he said, "He cried and I felt bad."

What's the difference between these two boys? Richard is an angry, aggressive boy who bullies his classmates at school. He often feels angry and frustrated, and acts out without concern for what might happen next or how anyone might feel. Sam is well adjusted and socially competent. He rarely hits others, because he's able to find different ways to express his feelings. But even he experiences rare moments when he loses control.

Children like Sam, who care about their own feelings, have empathy for those of others, and can resolve everyday conflicts that come up are more successful and better able to get along with people than children like Richard, who can't.

When children understand themselves and others, they are also able to:

- Wait for what they want
- Cope with the frustration when they can't get what they want
- Get along better with their peers
- Control their impulses and aggression
- Resist peer pressure

But the benefits of social and emotional competence don't stop there. Children who are aware of their own feelings and feel sympathy—even empathy—for others may be able to stop themselves from attacking another because they feel, or at least understand, another's pain. And they may also wish to help another already in distress *if* they have the problem-solving skills to do that. These children are more likely to share and take turns, and display other pro-social behaviors, such as cooperation. Good problem solvers are more resilient and less likely to withdraw from people and problems they can't solve. They are better able to stand up for themselves, and less fearful of peers.

As Leonard Eron and L. Rowell Huesmann inform us, children who do not learn pro-social behaviors are likely to become anti-social later on. Because socially withdrawn children don't cause trouble or disrupt the classroom, they often go unnoticed. They *must not* go unnoticed. Unable or unwilling to express their feelings and solve everyday problems, socially withdrawn children may hold their feelings in. As Kenneth Rubin has reported, these skill deficits may cause children to become depressed in the future—or, as suggested by Melvin Lee and others, to engage in violent behaviors. Social withdrawal is not something that one outgrows naturally. These youngsters need the very attention they shrink from.

Raising a Thinking Preteen is for preteens like Richard who are having trouble getting along with others, whether at school or at home, and for those who, like Sam, are thriving, but need to hone their problem-solving skills. No matter how good at problem solving children may already be, they can always become even better. ICPS can also help children with Attention Deficit Hyperactivity Disorder (ADHD), as Bonnie Aberson has learned, and can be adapted for children far more volatile than Richard, as illustrated by Ross Greene in his informative book *The Explosive Child*.

Throughout the book you'll find a step-by-step conflict resolution plan for you and your child.

Why Are the Years
Eight to Twelve Important?

"Isn't an eight-year-old too young to be considered a preteen?" you may be asking yourself. Not anymore. The reality is that children are growing up faster than ever, and fourth and fifth grades are nothing short of watershed years.

Physically, children mature earlier than they did even a generation ago. Studies indicate that the first physical signs of puberty can be detected in girls at about age seven, and in boys, about two years later. Even the average age at which girls reach menarche has dropped.

Behaviorally and emotionally, research indicates that problems begin to peak during fourth and fifth grades.

Academically, children now leave the cocoon of elementary school a year or two earlier than they did a generation ago. As a result, teachers begin preparing students for middle school as early as third grade. They assign more longer-range projects which require students to assume more responsibility for finishing their projects and budgeting their time.

Socially, children become increasingly self-conscious and aware of their peer group by the time they turn eight. They sense that the larger world is opening up to them, a prospect that both enlivens and intimidates them.

These intervening years between early childhood and adolescence, all but ignored as a "developmental phase" a generation ago, are emerging as a crucial time in children's lives. Children this age are very aware of the problems teenagers are dealing with, and they know that they will soon face similar situations in school, at home, and with their friends.

Even more serious, young children today sometimes face situations that threaten their future safety and well-being. For example, a recent survey by the national drug-prevention program P.R.I.D.E., Inc., of over 130,000 students in twenty-six states, reveals that while drug usage among high-schoolers has stabilized, it has risen among younger children: one out of ten students in grades six to twelve are monthly drug users.

Because puberty hasn't yet hit with its full force, eight- to twelve-year-olds are still a few years away from experiencing the natural rebellion of adolescence. They are still attached to their parents, open to guidance, and eager for help. The years from eight to twelve may seem like a narrow window of time, but it is long enough to enable parents and teachers to have an impact on the kind of teenagers their children will become.

These years are also a magical time when youngsters are beginning to come into their own and explore who they are in many new and exciting ways. According to my research colleague George Spivack, preadolescents value and evaluate themselves in terms of their appearance, their relationships with friends, school performance, and sports ability. In my view, children also come to value themselves in terms of their problem-solving ability.

Good problem solvers have a "can do" attitude. They feel as if they can make things happen, rather than experiencing the world as a place in which things happen to them. If they are selected as most valuable player on their soccer team, they don't conclude that they're naturally gifted, but remember all the time they spent practicing. If they do well in school, they don't attribute their good grades to easy tests and lax teachers, but to the fact that they studied hard.

It's also true that they probably do well because they are free to concentrate on the tasks at hand. Maurice Elias and his colleagues have shown that fifth-graders who learn problem-solving skills experience less stress during their transition from elementary to middle school. (These stresses include the logistics of transferring to a new school, adjusting to more stringent academic requirements, and coping with peer pressure.) In turn, these youngsters-in-transition stay on task and do better in school. On the other hand, Eric Dubow and John Tisak show us how youngsters who are impeded by emotional blocks have difficulty paying attention in school, and if they're not paying attention, they're not going to learn. These authors found that problem-solving skills help the children handle pressure from parents, teachers, and friends, which in turn helps them feel emotionally free to concentrate on their schoolwork. In this light, the years before adolescence are a time during which problem-solving skills can be particularly helpful in reducing stress.

But the salutary effects of ICPS are even more far-reaching. As children master the ICPS skills, they will be increasingly able to cope with a bully, balance their schoolwork with outside activities, and not only resist peer pressure, but experience more success in negotiating with peers and making friends. ICPS-competent preteens are able to bounce back from failure. They know what to do and how to do it. They don't give up too soon. Several studies, such as that by Patricia Morison and Ann Masten, indicate that children who engage in high-risk behaviors before their teen years are more likely to find themselves acting in ways which threaten their safety and well-being during their teen years.

- A 1982 study found that seventh graders who smoke cigarettes and have a rebellious attitude are at risk for nine different types of substance abuse by ninth grade.

• A 1987 review of a series of studies indicates that aggression and withdrawn behaviors evidenced during the preteen years not only persist as children grow, but are also reliable predictors that more serious problems—a tendency toward violence, substance abuse, teen pregnancy, becoming a school dropout, and inability to hold a job—will develop later.

It follows that if we can teach children to think about their options before they become teenagers, they will be less likely to encounter trouble in the years ahead.

To help prepare our preteens for the tumultuous yet exciting adolescent years, let's help those who are just learning problem-solving skills to become good problem solvers, and those who are already "ICPSers" to become even better. They will then have the skills they need to feel safe when they begin to navigate the myriad changes they will soon face.

As research has indicated, children showing behaviors that put them at high risk for developing later problems can come from urban or rural neighborhoods, or the suburbs. They can come from poor families or wealthy ones, any race or ethnic origin.

In fact, the ICPS method has been adopted by school districts and mental health agencies in states across the country, including Alabama, Delaware, Florida, Georgia, Illinois, New Jersey, Pennsylvania, Tennessee, Utah, and Virginia. ICPS has been recognized as an exemplary primary prevention program by the National Mental Health Association, and by three task forces of the American Psychological Association. More recently, it was recognized as an exemplary prevention program by the National Association of School Psychologists, the Office of Juvenile Justice and Delinquency Prevention, and the Substance Abuse and Mental Health Services Administration; it was also cited as one of the top six violence prevention programs by the Mid-Atlantic States region of the Office of Health and Human Services. In addition, it was cited as fostering emotional intelligence by the Collaborative for the Advancement of Social and Emotional Learning (CASEL), a national clearinghouse for prevention programs for children.

With its emphasis on primary prevention, *Raising a Thinking Preteen* can help kids behave differently—because they will learn to think differently. It can help your child, too.

◀ 1 ▶

Kids Who Behave Differently Think Differently

It is just as important to solve "people" problems as it is to solve problems in math.

Between the ages of eight and twelve, children go through sweeping physical, social, emotional, and cognitive transitions. Confusingly, changes in these different areas often don't keep pace with each other. It's not uncommon to meet sixth-graders who look like eighth-graders but act and think like fifth-graders.

Children also differ dramatically in how they approach a problem. Consider four twelve-year-old boys. One may feel rejected if a friend declines an invitation to come home with him after school and play video games. Another may be the kind of kid who doesn't take "no" for an answer and reacts by threatening his friend. The third, when faced with a firm refusal, may try to find another way to entice his friend into changing his mind, and is therefore less likely to give up hope. And the fourth may ask his friend why he declined the invitation, consider the answer, and ask again using the new information.

The way a child reacts to typical social problems, like declined invitations, is important. Children who have interpersonal problem-solving skills tend to thrive. Children who lack these skills may develop social problems later on.

How parents react to these typical problems also has an impact. Some parental reactions guide behavior in positive, healthy ways; others do not. In the next chapter, we'll look at various ways parents handle their children's conflicts, and how they can help their children to develop special problem-solving skills.

Now let's meet three children and compare how they react when they have to solve problems. These three children, and the others highlighted in this book, are composites of many youngsters with whom I have worked; however, all the situations and dialogues are real.

Nicholas, age ten, is very popular with his peers. Not only does he have many play dates after school, but he's sought after in school as well: his classmates want him to be on their team for cooperative class projects, and on their sports teams too. Once in a while he may lose his temper, or express impatience—especially with his eight-year-old sister—but generally he's able to control his angry outbursts. And for the most part, he's learned to cope with the frustration of not always getting what he wants the minute he wants it.

Sarah, age eleven, wants others to play with her, but is rejected by her peers—she neither asks for nor receives help from them. She behaves aggressively when she wants something and flies off the handle when things don't go her way. Typical of many aggressive girls, as described by Suellen and Paula Fried, and by Carla Garrity and her colleagues, Sarah's bullying tactics are more verbal than physical. She yells at others, argues with them, and threatens them if they don't give her what she wants. If sufficiently provoked, she may also attack in physical ways. In class she's frequently disruptive, and resorts to lying.

Donna, a very bright nine-year-old, wants to have friends and play with others. No one really dislikes her—they just don't know she's there. Donna stands around watching, waiting for children to invite her to play, unable to figure out how to secure such an invitation. Soon, she gives up and walks away. Her feelings are hurt.

Research by John Coie, Jens Asendorpf, and their colleagues inform us that some timid or shy children like Donna are not actively rejected as much as they are simply ignored. They may be afraid to join others, and afraid to answer questions out loud when called upon in school by their teacher. It's especially difficult for shy preteens. Often, they give up trying to relate successfully to others, to express their feelings, and to stand up for their rights.

Before training these children and their parents in the "I Can Problem Solve" (ICPS) program, I wanted to assess their skills as problem solvers. To do this, I asked them to consider several kinds of social situations children might find themselves in. I wanted to determine how skilled they were in the five ICPS skills mentioned in the introduction: understanding another's point of view, understanding motives, finding alternative solutions, considering consequences, and sequenced planning.

ICPS Skill #1: Understanding Another's Feelings and Point of View

To understand how, and if, the children were sensitive to and aware of people's feelings, I asked each of the three to draw a picture of two children: one sad, and one not sad. Giving no further information, I asked them to make up a story about the two characters.

Nicholas's story went like this:

Corey (not-sad boy) asked Bert (sad boy) what was wrong.
Bert said, "My dog's going to die."
Corey said, "I'm sure your dog will be all right."

Bert cried even harder and said, "No he won't. A car ran over him."

"Yes, I know," Corey said, "but they took him to a very good vet and he's doing surgery on him."

"But Corey, the car hit his head."

Corey tried to make him feel better. He told Bert, "But not hard enough to damage anything."

But Bert was still sad. "But what if he dies. What will I do?"

Corey said, "First of all, he's not going to die. Second of all, whatever does happen, your family and me will be here to help. So let's go inside and wait for the vet to call."

"Thanks, Corey."

In this fictitious situation, Nicholas created a boy who understood and sympathized with the feelings of another, even though he did not experience those emotions himself. Through Corey, Nicholas was able to step outside of himself and focus on Bert's needs, not his own.

Sarah, who drew two girls, described their conversation a different way:

Missy is the happy girl and Buffy is sad. Buffy told Missy, "I lost the championship. I threw the ball and no one caught it and we lost the game."

Missy told her, "Don't worry. You already won one."

"But this one was different. It was more important to me. It's my last game in the league."

Missy tells her not to feel bad—she can win a championship next year, and then says, "Didn't you hate those hamburgers we had for lunch? They were really dry."

Sarah identified why Buffy was sad. But in her story, Missy, instead of listening to Buffy explain why she wasn't comforted—

because this was her last game in the league—ignored Buffy's explanation and said that Buffy could win a championship next year. Missy avoided dealing with Buffy's sadness, dismissed her explanation, and then changed the subject.

Donna depicted the two girls as sisters. Here is her story:

The one that's crying is Maddie; she's nine years old. Her twelve-year-old sister Liza is making her feel bad, telling her that their parents love her more, and Maddie believes her. Maddie locks herself in her room. Her parents try to get her out to get something to eat. Her parents ask, "What's wrong?" and she says, "Liza said you love her more than me."

They say, "No, that's not true. We love you both equally." And then Maddie feels okay.

It is interesting that Donna portrayed the not-sad girl as being the one who made the other one feel sad. Sometimes creating stories provides a shy child with the opportunity to express inner thoughts that she would not be able to express in real life.

To sum up how the three children dealt with a character who felt sad, Nicholas depicted a child actively trying to help another in distress, Sarah's character avoided sadness, and Donna let someone else (Maddie's parents) undo the sadness that the not-sad sister had instigated.

ICPS Skill #2: Understanding Motives

To gauge the children's depth of understanding as to why people might do what they do, I created a character who was always off by himself, showing no interest in playing with others. I told the children, "This child doesn't seem to want any friends. Why might a child not want to have friends?"

Typical of a socially competent child Nicholas's age, he understood that people might do things for a variety of reasons, and easily generated many explanations. Interestingly, they fell into one of two categories. In the first were those that take into account superficial, external motives, such as, "He just doesn't like anybody, so nobody likes him."

But he was also able to look below the surface and list several motives that weren't so obvious: "Maybe his father is poor and he doesn't want to be embarrassed and doesn't want his kid to be embarrassed either," or "He thinks people use him all the time."

Sarah, like many aggressive children her age, focused on a more superficial reason: "She's got all this stuff and doesn't want anybody to take it away from her."

Donna, like Nicholas, was able to see beneath the surface, "Maybe people are always hurting her feelings," but, like Sarah, generated a limited repertoire of possibilities. This inability to think of a variety of reasons people might do what they do can prevent her from having a greater understanding of how someone might really be feeling, how to help that person feel better, and how to relate to those feelings when she finds herself in a conflict with that person.

As I will discuss in Chapter 5, understanding why people behave the way they do at a given moment may not always be the same as understanding why someone behaves the same way consistently over time.

ICPS Skill #3:
Finding Alternative Solutions

To learn how flexible Nicholas was in his thinking when faced with a problem between two people, I asked him to consider this hypothetical situation: "Johnny asked Daniel to play ball with him, but Daniel refused. What can Johnny do to get Daniel to play ball with him?"

"Ask him," Nicholas said.

"That's one possibility," I said. "Can you think of another?"

Nicholas came up with seven additional solutions. He suggested that Johnny could:

- Wait till Daniel's not doing anything and maybe he'll get bored
- Tell Daniel he'll get lots of kids to play and they can all play together
- Offer to help Daniel with his homework and then ask him to play
- Just drop a hint and Daniel will catch on
- Show Daniel how to play hoops
- Challenge him to a game of hoops and let him win
- Hypnotize him to sleep and then suggest they play

Most socially and emotionally competent children who are well liked by their peers are able, as Nicholas was, to think of seven or eight different ways to solve this type of problem.

Both Sarah and Donna (given girls' names for the above scenario) were unable to think of more than three or four solutions to this problem. They tended to offer many different variations on a common theme. For example, one of Sarah's solutions was to ask, "Why won't you play with me? I would play with you." She then offered a second solution: "I'll invite you to my party." Perseverating on the same theme, she said next, "I'll invite you to my house," and "I'll take you to the movies." Although Sarah thought of inviting the girl to a different place each time, each solution used the theme of "inviting." In the end, Sarah could only think of two different solutions.

Donna was able to generate three solutions. She tried hard to think of ways to get the other child to play ball, and said, "Tell her she'll be her friend," "Help her if she gets in trouble," and "Tell her they'd play a girl's game." She also came up with variations on the last solution of doing something with the ball: "Tell her they could play volleyball," and "Let's play catch."

ICPS Skill #4:
Considering Consequences

To see how well these children could think about the impact of their behavior on themselves and others, I made up this situation: Johnny (or Ruth) wanted the ball Daniel (or Loni) was playing with, and stole it. I then asked the children to think of all the different things that might happen next. Nicholas thought of many consequences, and significantly, they were of two different types. The first type were those which I call *external* consequences, because they are imposed by others:

- Johnny might get in trouble
- Johnny might get beaten up when the other boy finds out
- Daniel might spread rumors about him
- Daniel might steal his money
- Daniel might say, "Now you can NEVER play with my ball!"

But he also realized that actions can have a psychological impact on both perpetrator and victim, outcomes which I call *internal* consequences:

- Daniel will feel sad that someone took his ball
- Daniel will worry about what happened to his ball
- Johnny might feel bad if he upset someone

These internal consequences indicate that Nicholas understood that actions affect how other people feel, and that he could empathize with others.

Sarah was also able to think about what might happen next after Ruth took Loni's soccer ball, but she thought about external consequences to the perpetrator, not empathic consequences to the victim.

• Ruth will get in trouble
• Loni will tell the teacher
• Loni will steal something of hers
• Loni will call her stupid

Sarah then perseverated on the same theme of the last consequence. She added, "Loni will tell Ruth, 'You can't play soccer anyway,'" and "Loni will tell Ruth she's a dork." Both of these are variations of calling her "stupid" because they're all forms of belittling.

Perhaps Sarah has experienced these consequences in real life, but it hasn't stopped her from behaving aggressively. Perhaps she has become immune to these kinds of consequences, or perhaps she continues her aggressive ways because they get her what she wants. Or maybe she simply can't think of what else to do.

Donna, who as we saw before is aware of others' feelings, said, "Loni might start to cry." Although Donna was able to think of a more empathic consequence than Sarah was, she was unable to generate more possibilities, which prevented her from thinking further about this act of transgression.

Sympathy (feeling bad about another in pain) and empathy (feeling another's pain) are not skills in themselves, but they are important attributes that affect how well people can solve problems. Children who can generate a range of possible solutions and consider them in light of how they will make another person feel can become good problem solvers.

ICPS Skill #5: Sequenced Planning

Similarly, children who can take the feelings of others into account while planning ahead to reach a goal will become skilled problem solvers. To assess the children's ability to do this, I suggested that they tell me a story about something very important to them—making friends. I told them to think about how a child who had just moved into a new neighborhood would go about making friends, and asked them to tell me everything that happens. This technique, developed by George Spivack and Murray Levine for use with adolescents, assesses a person's spontaneous ability to plan sequenced steps toward an interpersonal goal, to anticipate potential obstacles that could interfere with reaching that goal, and to realize that problem solving may take time.

Nicholas told his story this way:

> First Al got talking to the leader (the most popular boy in the group). He found out the kids liked basketball, but Al didn't know how to play. When Al got to know the leader better, he asked him to get the kids down to the skating rink. The kids went and saw him practicing shooting goals. So the kids asked him, "Would you teach us how to do that?" So he did, and they organized two teams and the kids liked that and Al had lots of friends.

Like other socially competent children, Nicholas is skilled at *sequenced planning*. His plan included a two-step sequence (talking to the leader and finding out what the kids liked to play)—interrupted by an obstacle (Al didn't know how to play the game the kids liked)—followed by a recognition that it takes time to make new friends (when Al got to know the leader better). He even added another step to reach his goal—interesting them in another sport.

I asked Sarah to create the same story, about a girl named Anita.

Anita saw lots of kids in a group on the playground. She asked them to play frisbee and they said yes. They threw the frisbee, and they laughed and they got tired running so far to get the frisbee. They really could throw it far.

Notice that Sarah's story had no sequenced steps. Rather, she offered one isolated solution—asking the group to play frisbee. Her approach to the problem was to move directly to the goal without considering how best to get there. She recognized neither that potential obstacles might interfere with her goal, nor that making friends might take time. In fact, most of her story described activities that occurred *after* the goal was reached.

The actual story Sarah related contained no negative, forceful content. Yet Sarah behaves in an aggressive manner in real life. How do I reconcile this apparent contradiction? It isn't so much *what* Sarah thinks as *how* she thinks. The goal of the story was to make friends, and Sarah jumped directly to the goal, without any recognition of how long it takes to make friends. This indicates how impulsive her thinking is. But in addition to her lack of planning skills, she fails to take into account the feelings of other people. Taken together, this gap in her skills prevents her from relating successfully with others in her life. This is what I mean when I say that behavior is guided not by what children think, but how. The *process* of their thinking is more associated with their behavior than with the content of the thought.

The extent to which Donna feels unable to overcome her shyness is apparent in the story I asked her to tell me about how fictional Anita might go about making friends.

Anita introduced herself to the kids at school. She waited until someone asked her to play, but they didn't, and

Anita was sad. But then one girl asked her to play. So now Anita had lots of friends, and she wasn't lonely anymore. They played together and they laughed a lot and now Anita's happy 'cause she has lots of friends.

Donna was adept at the skill of recognizing Anita's feelings—sadness, then happiness—and expressed sensitivity as to why she felt the way she did. She was also able to recognize an obstacle: not being asked to play. And she did mention time: "She waited." However, like many children who cannot join groups, Donna had poor planning skills. Because she was so passive, she ended up waiting too long, and this made her feel sad. Notice also that Anita herself did nothing to change her circumstances; she went from not being asked to play to being asked, but provided no steps as to how that happened. Her friends simply approached her, as if by magic.

Like Sarah, Donna's story lacked sequenced steps. Unlike Sarah, however, her only strategy (introducing herself) was met with an obstacle. But in both stories, no plan of action was created.

Though this skill resembles *alternative solution* thinking, it's actually more complex. Alternative solution skills require the ability to think of different, unconnected solutions. Sequenced planning involves insight and forethought to prevent or circumvent potential obstacles from arising and, in addition, having alternative plans if an obstacle proves realistically or psychologically insurmountable. The process implies an awareness that goals are not always reached immediately. Another aspect of time, which will be addressed in a later chapter, is an understanding that certain times are more advantageous than others for taking action (for example, it's a good idea to wait for someone to be in a good mood before asking her for a favor).

Using ICPS Skills in Real Life

Nicholas, a good problem solver, is far better able to call on his ICPS skills in real life than are Sarah or Donna.

When a friend called Nicholas at the last minute to tell him he was sick and couldn't go to the movies, Nicholas thought about telling him to come anyway because they had a ride already arranged—his father left work early to take them. But before speaking, he realized that he was only thinking of himself. So he told his friend he hoped he'd feel better, and to call him when he was well. Then, instead of just moping around the house, he called another friend, invited him to the movie, and the friend said yes.

Let's look at Nicholas's plan. First, Nicholas *thought* about what he wanted to say, and realized he was not showing concern about his friend's feelings or the fact that he was sick. Instead of flying off the handle with frustration, he trusted that his friend did not make this up, and that he really did want to go. Nicholas also recognized that this was not a good time to nag his friend to go (a part of *sequenced planning*). He then thought of a solution to accommodate his father, who was en route, by calling another friend.

Sarah's inability to problem solve has repercussions in her life. She told me about a time she invited a classmate to play with her after school, and the girl told her that her mother wanted to take her shopping. Having been refused so many times before, Sarah assumed her classmate didn't have to go shopping with her mother, and threatened her by exclaiming, "You'll be sorry. I'm going to get you after school. You won't be able to go shopping with your mother!"

Why would Sarah make such an ominous comment? It's not that she couldn't think of consequences. Like other aggressive children, she was able to imagine what would happen next— perhaps she'd be threatened in return, chastised by the girl's parents, or even permanently rejected. But that awareness didn't stop her from threatening her classmate, even though she knew she wouldn't actually carry it out. I believe she simply didn't know what else to do. Because of her limited planning skills and her inability to foresee alternative solutions and take another's perspective, she resorted to a strategy (the threat) that had the exact opposite outcome from the one she wanted.

In real life, Donna, like Sarah, is handicapped by her inability to think of solutions to her problems. She told me about a time when she bumped into another child while in line, and that child told the teacher on her. She accurately concluded that the child was angry at her, yet she was unable to take the next step and try to remedy the situation. Not knowing how to approach the girl and redress the wrong, Donna froze. She became even more fearful of the other girl.

Clearly, being aware of and sensitive to others' feelings are crucial to problem solving. In fact, emotional awareness and sensitivity are prerequisites to problem-solving skills, because they enable us to think of different ways to solve conflicts. But they are not sufficient. We still need to have specific problem-solving skills. As Donna has shown us, we have to know what to do about another's anger in order to relieve our anxiety.

Both Sarah and Donna want friends, yet they don't know how to accomplish their goal—Sarah chases her friends away; Donna fades into invisibility.

Neither Sarah nor Donna does well in school, although they both have the ability to achieve. Donna is a good example of how a very bright child with a capacity for academic success does not always achieve that success. The girls' preoccupation with making friends blocks them from concentrating on their work. They are consumed with their longing to have friends, to be popular, but have no idea how to make this happen. Success in the impersonal world of academic achievement often depends on success in the interpersonal world of social and emotional competence.

Although Sarah's and Donna's behaviors are still in the "normal" range, they display more than average amounts of disconcerting behaviors. My research has shown that ICPS can help children like Sarah and Donna learn to make responsible decisions and to feel pride in their successes instead of frustration in their failures.

Some very socially adjusted children are not as competent with ICPS as Nicholas, and some aggressive and withdrawn children are more competent than Sarah and Donna. But the many hundreds of children I have worked with have shown that similar patterns of behavior are generally accompanied by the styles of thinking in the interpersonal arena that I have described.

Why Does Nicholas Need ICPS?

Although Nicholas is already an emotionally competent child and a skilled problem solver, he can still benefit from ICPS training for several reasons. First, there's no ceiling or upper limit when it comes to learning interpersonal skills. Even the most skilled children can always hone their skills and become better. Nicholas often finds himself provoked by his younger sister, for example. Other times, he doesn't listen to his parents. He can't always follow through when it comes to translating his thoughts into deeds. In all these situations, Nicholas can learn to rely on ICPS more than he already does.

It's also true that the people Nicholas encounters in his daily life may not be as skilled as he is. He will naturally run into other children, and even adults, who say hurtful things or thwart his desires. Conflicts with siblings, parents, and kids at school are a very normal part of growing up, but being a good "ICPSer" will make the journey more pleasant, and more successful. My goal is not to eliminate conflict, but to help children learn to cope with it, to help them appreciate how others think and feel about things, and to build their skills to solve the problems that result from conflict.

Some well-adjusted children may be very skilled in one ICPS area, such as being able to create a sequenced plan toward a goal, but significantly less skilled when it comes to figuring out what may interfere with the plan, how long their plan may take, or when is the best time to enact the plan. Other well-adjusted children may be so skilled at thinking of possible obstacles that they can't act at all. They tend to become paralyzed by thoughts like, "That won't work because. . . ." These children can only benefit from learning ICPS.

Finally, ICPS is an excellent program of prevention. Even children like Nicholas can fall prey to later problems, including being subjected to unwanted peer pressure, becoming the victim of a bully, or experimenting with drugs. My research has shown that children trained in ICPS—whether as preschoolers or pre-teens—are more likely to remain socially and emotionally competent than some of their peers without this advantage, perhaps because ICPS training helps to reinforce and perpetuate the ability to make good decisions.

All children, no matter how skilled they are, will face new and unexpected challenges as they grow, and their parents won't always be there to protect them. Parents who let their children know that they value *thinking* about what to do and say will raise children who will be more likely to use the ICPS skills when they need them.

My goal is for children to maximize their problem-solving skills, to know how and when to act, to gain control of their lives, and to grow up to be thinking, feeling human beings who are able to make good decisions.

Now, let's look at how parents can foster these skills.

◀ 2 ▶

Four Styles of Parenting

*If we change the way we talk to kids, it will change the
way they talk to us, to other kids, and to themselves.*

What do parents say when they want to change their child's
behavior? After listening to and studying parents' approaches for years, I've concluded that much of the time they
resort to one of three strategies: they use power, suggestions, or
explanations.

Obviously, not everything we say or do when we are trying
to change our children's behavior falls into one of these categories. There are also times when we use two or three of these
approaches at once. Still, examining our behavior through this
broad lens is useful. It will help us to see how the Problem-
Solving Approach, which I introduced in *Raising a Thinking
Child*, has its own unique importance for eight- through twelve-
year-olds.

Let's look at the three approaches parents most com-
monly use.

The Power Approach

Parents who use this approach think they can influence their children's behavior by being strong and imposing their will. They think of themselves as authoritarian, and often:

- Yell, as if sheer volume will command a child's attention
- Use belittling, humiliating put-downs, such as, "You are so stupid to do that again!"
- Ask repetitive, rhetorical questions, such as "How many times do I have to tell you . . . !"
- Use physical punishment, whether a slap on the wrist or spanking

The Power Approach may subdue children, but it strips them of their sense of personal power, and makes them angry and frustrated instead of proud of what they are doing. Because all human beings need to feel as if they have a sense of control over their lives, children who don't experience control at home look elsewhere. Often, they seek power in a safer environment, like school, where they act toward other children as they are treated at home. As Murray Straus and Brian Barber explain, this is one reason children become aggressive. Children of parents who belittle them believe that the way to feel strong—to become as powerful as their parents—is by diminishing the power of others. Although all children whose parents use the Power Approach do not turn out to be aggressive, psychologists like George Batsche describe how most aggressive children do have parents who primarily use the power approach.

Furthermore, yelling and spanking send a message to children that these are acceptable means of expression. Sarah's dad heard her screaming at her four-year-old brother and calling him names for "bugging" her to play while she was doing her homework. Her dad yelled, "How many times do I have to tell you not to talk to your brother that way! Now go to your room and think about what you're doing!" If Sarah was thinking at all, it was probably about how to get revenge. Or perhaps she was wondering why it was all right for her father to yell at her, but not all right for her to yell at her brother. In her room, she may well conclude that even though her father tells her not to yell, yelling is okay.

Most likely, however, Sarah wasn't thinking at all. She was probably feeling self-protective, wanting to shut out her father's screams. What he actually said didn't matter to her; the words became jumbled together into a verbal assault.

In the short run, this kind of discipline may seem effective— Sarah may well end up complying and stop calling her brother names. But the fact that she may outwardly change is less important than *why* she changes. Inwardly, she didn't have a change of heart—she still didn't understand why she shouldn't yell, and hadn't begun to explore her feelings or her brother's. She merely stopped yelling because she didn't want to be yelled at. Parents who use the Power Approach seem to accomplish their goal, but often at a very high cost that leaves everyone feeling angry, powerless, and frustrated.

Some children react differently to the assertion of power: they become immune, acting as if they don't fear punishment at all. Getting what they want or relieving frustration by venting anger is so important that they learn to endure any temporary pain to achieve those ends. Once they reach this stage, their behavior may become completely impossible to control. The verbal barrage and anger unleashed by Sarah's father would have no impact on her. She'd ignore it.

Think about the implications of this. If she doesn't care about being yelled at, how could she possibly care about how her brother feels when she yells at him? The Power Approach can actually prevent children from developing empathy—and empathy, as we will soon see, is a prerequisite for learning problem-solving skills. In fact, all meaningful behavior change is rooted in a child's ability to be empathic. Tellingly, most aggressive children do not feel empathy.

Other children may react to the Power Approach in a different way. Like Donna, they may simply withdraw, afraid to act at all. Even when the Power Approach is used in a "loving" way, children do not always experience the warmth their parents intend. For example, from the time she was in preschool, Donna's father tried to temper his spankings by simultaneously telling her, "I love you." As we will see, it was the power that Donna heard; his saying "I love you" only confused her. In the end, she felt as unempowered as Sarah.

The Suggesting Approach

Some parents, upon seeing their children in conflict, will make suggestions. If Sarah's dad had used this approach when his daughter yelled at her brother, he might have said, "Just ask him nicely to leave you alone," or "Tell your brother you're doing your homework and you'll play with him later." Now, these are perfectly reasonable suggestions. The problem isn't with what Sarah's father is saying. The real problem with the Suggesting Approach is that parents are thinking for their kids.

Eight-year-old Joanne, for example, comes home every day pouting because her friend Rita won't play with her. Eager to help, Joanne's mom says, "Why don't you tell her that you'll invite her to go swimming?" When Joanne reports that Rita doesn't want to go swimming, her mother, unwilling to give up, says, "Maybe she'd like to come over and we'll rent a video." But what happens if Rita doesn't want to do that either? Joanne may feel as if she's out of options. And in the face of her mother's suggestions, she had no opportunity to come up with ideas of her own.

The Suggesting Approach is also used frequently when problems come up between parents and their children. When kids balk at doing chores, for example, many parents simply suggest, "Try doing them as soon as you get home from school and get them out of the way." Often, children respond by whining, "I have to do my homework first or it will get too late." Parents who interpret this as back talk will often revert to the Power Approach. Meanwhile, the chores remain undone.

It's true that offering occasional suggestions can be helpful to a child facing a new situation. However, when parents actively think of solutions, children remain passive. If used too often, this approach can stifle a child's thinking process, self-expression, and emotions. Some children may react by blindly seeking and adopting the advice of others without thinking it through, while others, like Sarah, may choose aggressive solutions when Mom or Dad isn't around. Though the Suggesting Approach is more positive than the Power Approach, children are more likely to act on their own solutions if they are given the skills and the freedom to do so.

The Explaining Approach

Many parents realize that merely suggesting a course of action to their child isn't sufficient, so they work hard at offering explanations. Sometimes Nicholas's mom would say, "Your sister feels angry when you talk to her like that," and "I feel angry when you talk to your sister like that."

Using "I messages" to explain things to children, as advanced by Thomas Gordon in his classic book, *Parent Effectiveness Training*, is very popular today, and many parenting experts recommend it. While it's certainly less guilt-inducing than statements like "You're making him feel bad," it's ultimately ineffective, because again parents are taking the active role and kids are remaining passive. They're not being invited into the conversation, but asked to simply listen. And even though Nicholas's mom is talking to her son about feelings—an important part of problem solving—she's doing all the talking, and no one's listening.

I have also heard many parents say they do not punish their children when they misbehave, but rather, they talk to them about what they have done. One mom said, "I never spank or yell at my daughter; I reason with her." When I asked her for an example, she said, "When Mia gets into fights at school, I tell her she won't have any friends." Yet Mia still gets into fights.

Similarly, nine-year-old Jeff sometimes gets so angry when his younger brother plays with his model airplanes that Jeff hits him. Then Jeff's father says, "If you hit your brother, you might hurt him," or, "Your brother feels sad when you hit him."

Jeff always nods as if he understands, but he continues to hit his brother. Jeff's father and Mia's mother are perplexed. They can't understand why their kids don't change their behavior. But this illustrates a second problem with the Explaining Approach: parents are never sure if their message gets through.

Finally, the Explaining Approach falls short because kids eventually tune out. They begin to feel as if they've heard every explanation a thousand times, so they don't have to listen. In the end, though this approach is more sophisticated than the Suggesting Approach, it's just as ineffective.

The Problem-Solving Approach

What differentiates the Problem-Solving Approach from the others I've described is that it involves children in the process of thinking about what they're doing, and why. Children don't tune out when they're part of the conversation.

Let's return to Mia and Jeff for a moment. Suppose that one day, after Mia tells her mother that she got in a fight at school, her mother tries a new tack. Instead of offering her usual commentary—"If you hit kids, you won't have any friends"—she asks, "What do you think the girls might say or do after you hit them?"

Instead of saying, "Your brother feels sad when you hit him," what if Jeff's father asks, "How do you think your brother feels when you hit him?" or "Can you think of a different way to tell your brother how you feel when he takes something of yours without permission?"

Now both children are less likely to vacantly nod and remove themselves from the conversation. The questions posed to them encourage and guide them to become active participants in the discussion. In other words, the Problem-Solving Approach is the only one that allows parents and children to engage in true dialogues rather than monologues.

Joanne's mother, who suggested ways that her daughter could invite classmates to play with her, shifted to the Problem-Solving Approach. She asked Joanne to come up with ideas herself. One afternoon, Joanne came home beaming, "Mommy, Rita played with me today."

"What did you do?" her mom asked.

"I showed her the double twist and she wanted me to teach her how." How proud Joanne felt when she came up with an idea of her own!

Now let's compare the effectiveness of these four approaches with another problem between a dad and his eleven-year-old son, Derrick, who wants a ten-speed bike. The conversation starts out with Explanations about why he can't have it, and a Suggestion about what he can do instead.

Derrick: Chip got a ten-speed bike today.
Father: Yeah.
Derrick: When am I going to get mine?
Father: We've talked about this before. You're too young.
Derrick: I'm older than Chip.
Father: Chip is bigger than you and maybe he can handle it.
Derrick: I can ride a bike better than him.
Father: You have a very nice bike now. Why don't you ride the bike you have with your other friends?
Derrick: I want to ride with Chip.

(So much for this approach. Even though this father asked "Why . . . ?" he was not really asking a question. He was telling his son what *he* thought he should do.)

Father: Listen, ten-speed bikes are too big and too fast to ride on a little street like ours with all the cars. It's just too dangerous. I try to get you everything I can afford but this is just too dangerous for a guy your size. When you are older and bigger I will get you one.

(Derrick, having tuned out, didn't hear a word of this. He only heard "I can't have my bike.")

Derrick: You never get me anything!
Father: Don't talk back to me. I told you why you can't have one now and I don't want to hear any more about it.

Like many parents who engage in long explanations and suggestions, Derrick's father felt exasperated because "Derrick never listens." Feeling angry and frustrated, he shut down the conversation completely. And Derrick felt angry and frustrated too.

Now here's what happened when Derrick's father learned to use the Problem-Solving Approach.

Father: I know you want a ten-speed bike now, but I want you to think about this and I'm going to help you.

Derrick: Are you going to get me one?

Father: Yes, but not yet. Can you think of a reason why I don't want you to ride a ten-speed now?

Derrick: NO!

Father: Are you and Chip the same size or a different size?

Derrick: Different. He's bigger. But I can ride better than him.

Father: I know you think that. What might happen if you ride a bike that's too big and too fast on these little streets with lots of cars?

Derrick: Nothing. I'll be very careful.

Father: How do you know you'll never lose your concentration even for one second? What could happen then?

Derrick: I could fall and get hurt.

Father: And how would you feel if that happened?

Derrick: Sad.

Father: And how would Mom and I feel if that happened?

Derrick: Sad.

Father: And what else could happen?

Derrick: I could get hit by a car.

Father: Do you want that to happen?

Derrick: No.

Father: What can you do now so you won't fall and get hurt, or even get hit by a car?

Derrick: Wait till I'm older. Dad, maybe I could ride a three-speed now. That's still better than the old bike I have now.

Father: That's an idea. We'll go to the bike shop and look at them, and if it's safe, that will be a good solution to the problem.

Instead of suggesting and explaining, this father involved his son in thinking the problem through. By being asked to evaluate potential consequences, Derrick understood them—because he thought of them himself. And instead of ultimately shutting Derrick out of the discussion, the father listened to his son's solution, and was willing to accept it if it seemed safe.

By asking thoughtful questions, Derrick's father used the Problem-Solving Approach to its best advantage. He helped his son focus on four important skills that all good problem solvers need:

- Sensitivity to one's own feelings
- Sensitivity to others' feelings
- Awareness of *consequences* of behavior
- Recognition of possible *alternative solutions* to a problem

This kind of thinking also helped Derrick learn to wait for what he really wanted—which is an important life skill in itself. Overall, the dialogue left Derrick feeling proud of himself and his new solution. And his father was proud of him too.

Perhaps an old Chinese proverb has special meaning for us now:

> *Tell me, I forget.*
> *Teach me, I remember.*
> *Involve me, I understand.*

(And I'm not so sure about the remembering part.)

At first glance, it may seem that the Problem-Solving Approach is too complicated, and takes too long. But think for a moment about how long it takes for behavior to change if you don't use this approach—or if it changes at all. When Derrick's father was using the Explaining Approach, he said, "We talked about this before," suggesting that he's had an ongoing problem with his son. Yet once Derrick thought of a solution himself, his behavior changed almost immediately—and best of all, the change will probably last.

In the long run, using the Problem-Solving Approach saves time. Once the approach is mastered, the dialogues can be shortened. When Derrick, for example, wanted to stay out late on a school night with some friends, his father simply said, "Is that a good idea?" followed by, "Can you think of something different that is a good idea?" Within three minutes, Derrick was able to figure out a compromise solution.

Throughout this book, we will see how the parents of Nicholas, Sarah, and Donna learned to use the Problem-Solving Approach, one step at a time. By teaching your child how to make good decisions about problems important to them now, you are helping them prepare for problems that will be important to them later.

Understanding the importance of raising problem-solving children is the first step. In the next section, we'll explore how children ages eight to twelve can learn to think the problem-solving way.

Let's begin.

◀ 3 ▶

How Do I Feel?
How Do You Feel?

*Children have to care about their own feelings before
they can care about others'.*

Understanding how people feel about things is a very important part of solving the typical, everyday problems that
come up in our lives. To relieve someone's anger, frustration, or
fear, we have to first be aware of and sensitive to how they are
feeling. The only way we learn to pay attention to and take seriously the feelings of others is by first taking seriously and paying
attention to our own.

The way children act is grounded in how they feel. Before
they can make decisions with sensitivity to the emotions of
another, they have to be aware of and sensitive to how they feel
themselves. Emotional education, in other words, is a step-by-
step process. To ask a child to care about another person's feelings without first focusing on his own is like asking him to ride a
bicycle before having learned to ride a tricycle.

Several boys with whom I have worked frequently attacked
others physically to get what they wanted. All of them acknowledged that they often "got hit back," but one of them was quick
to add, "I don't care, I showed him who's boss." If boys like

these truly don't care, and have become immune to others' reactions to them, how can they possibly be concerned about the impact of their actions on other people?

Sarah, who uses verbal threats and barrages to intimidate others, is aware that others turn away from her, avoid playing with her, and don't want to be her friend. But like the boys who "don't care" what happens to them, she either does not think about or does not express how she feels about the reactions of those she upsets.

While being tuned in to and concerned about one's own feelings is an important first step, one must also be open to feeling another's pain. If Sarah becomes able to feel the pain of someone she torments or teases, and also feels sadness that she hurt someone else, she will be open to finding different ways to solve the problems that come up with her classmates.

Donna, like many shy youngsters, is aware of her own and others' feelings—she may know that something she did or said may have made another person angry—but because she doesn't know what to do about her anger, she retreats, and does nothing at all. In other words, she acts as if she didn't have the awareness she in fact possesses.

And what about Nicholas? Not only is he able to think about his own and others' feelings, but unlike Sarah and Donna, he has the problem-solving skills to know what to do about those feelings. Yet he doesn't always call upon those skills in the heat of emotion, especially when in conflict with his younger sister Tara, who, although not a behavior problem, is a little less socially and emotionally competent than her brother.

How Can Children Think
about Feelings?

All children experience a wide range of emotions early in life. What differs is whether they are able and willing to think about their feelings, and how they think about them.

Parents can encourage emotional awareness in many ways, but there's a very easy way all parents should try: ask children how they feel—when they are engaged in a conflict, when they receive a compliment, when they lose at a game, or when their best friend rejects them. This easy question sends a very important message to all children. It tells them, "I care about your feelings, and I want you to care about them too."

The more parents notice their children's feelings, the more children become aware of them. The degree to which children—and adults—are aware of their emotions varies greatly. Children learn about their emotions gradually. As I discussed in *Raising a Thinking Child*, by about age four, many children are able to understand that they, as well as others:

- Have feelings that can be identified and labeled
- Can feel different ways about the same thing at different times

These two dimensions of emotional awareness have an enormous impact on how children feel, think, and act.

By about age eight, children can also begin to understand a third, more sophisticated dimension of emotional awareness. They realize that they, as others:

- Can have contradictory, mixed feelings about something

An eight-year-old, for example, can feel sad that her grandma died, but is able to temper her feelings of loss with feelings of relief that she is no longer suffering. This helps her cope with her grief.

To sum up, children who appreciate that people can feel different ways about something at different times ("I feel sad now but I'll feel happy later," or "Mom is not always angry") can focus on the positive emotion to help get over a momentary hurt. Children who understand that they can have mixed emotions about something can focus on the good feelings as a way to overcome anxieties or fears. These skills then pave the way for children to understand that others may be experiencing the same emotional contrasts, and to help others in similar distress.

Who Should Participate?

All kids can benefit from talking about their feelings. Most parents know this about their daughters, but some question the fact when it comes to their sons. They worry that their sons will resist talking about their feelings with friends for fear of being teased or called names, and may shrink from it at home because "that's what girls do."

It's true that from birth, parents—especially mothers—are more emotionally expressive with their daughters than with their sons. It's also true that as children approach the preschool years, parents talk more about emotions (except for anger) with their daughters than their sons. Some believe their son must not show too much emotion or he will be perceived as a "mama's boy." However, in his book *Real Boys*, William Pollack reports that when parents don't talk to their sons about feelings, believing that "boys will be boys," their sons react by feeling anxious and sad— emotions they then feel compelled to hide. This vicious cycle of silence about emotions has to be broken. In my work with boys ranging in age from four to twelve, I have found that if asked about their feelings in calm, peaceful moments, they respond just as enthusiastically as girls. Emotional expression rather than repression helps both boys and girls to become thinking, feeling human beings who don't want to hurt themselves or others.

When talking to eight- to twelve-year-old boys and girls, I found that even the oldest still enjoyed talking about their feelings, and some still enjoyed this discussion in the context of a game.

Learning the Problem-Solving Approach

I suggest to all parents who are new to the Problem-Solving Approach that they begin with and focus on just one aspect of the approach at a time, and gradually put the pieces together.

Even though eight- to twelve-year-old children may know some or all of the feeling words they will need to help them solve problems, they do not always think about them in the heat of conflict. That's why it's useful to begin ICPS training with exercises that focus only on words that describe people's emotions—first about how *they* feel about things, and then how others (including their parents) feel. This gradual approach not only helps parents, who need time to feel comfortable with this new way of talking to kids, but helps kids accustom themselves to the new approach as well.

When to Begin

Families introduce feeling words at times convenient for them. Dinnertime was the perfect opportunity for Nicholas's family— everyone was together and the atmosphere was calm and peaceful. Sarah's parents also used dinnertime because they realized that talking about feelings often helped dissipate the sometimes tense atmosphere that arose at the end of the day. Donna's family found a different time. Because of her shyness, Donna preferred to talk about her feelings with one parent at a time, usually after dinner, and before tackling any unfinished homework.

Talking about Feeling Words

An easy way to begin is to say, "We're going to do some activities (or play some games) from a program called 'I Can Problem Solve.' We can call it ICPS for short." (Soon your children will ask for ICPS, and this phrase may become part of your household vernacular.)

> *Note*: If your children already know about ICPS from my book *Raising a Thinking Child*, you can simply say, "Remember the games we played that we called ICPS? Now we're going to play a new version of it, only it's a lot harder. Are you ready for the challenge?"

We'll start by reviewing several words that I covered in my earlier book—happy, sad, angry, afraid, proud, and frustrated. Some of these may be four-year-old words, but they are not four-year-old feelings. Eight- through twelve-year-olds still enjoy talking about them, and often have a whole new perspective on these feelings which often proves eye-opening to parents.

Begin with the word "happy." Ask your child:

- What makes *you* happy?
- What might make other people happy?

When Nicholas's mom asked him to name three things that made him happy, he replied immediately, "A new baseball mitt, chocolate cake, and our new puppy."

Wishing to include her daughter in the discussion, his mom turned to Tara and asked her the same question. Having heard Nicholas's answer, she repeated "Our new puppy," then added "blueberry pie," and "when daddy doesn't yell at me."

To make the game more challenging, their mom asked them, "What do you think would make both a grandmother and a ten-year-old feel happy?" Nicholas gleefully offered, "Getting a birthday card."

Nicholas and Tara were equally fluent with the words "sad," "angry," "afraid," "proud," and "frustrated." Tara especially enjoyed playing the memory game with the word "frustrated." She loved letting her parents know, in a safe way, that she feels frustrated when they make her go to bed before she's tired. And Tara and Nicholas also enjoyed thinking of people to pair, and talking about how they feel. Tara said that her friend's moving away made her *and* her friend feel sad, and Nicholas added that forgetting to say "thank you" when they give him something makes his grandmother *and* his teacher sad.

You can make up your own combinations of people, however unlikely—like a police officer and a four-year-old—and then let your children think of unusual combinations of people.

Donna also responded enthusiastically to these questions, even though she's so often emotionally withdrawn. But using the exercises in this way gave her parents an unexpected insight into her feelings. When she was asked what makes her happy, she replied, "When Mom says, 'I love you.'" Her mom grew a little embarrassed since her husband was sitting right there, so she asked, "How do you feel when Daddy says 'I love you'?" Donna replied, "That makes me sad," reminding her father that he often told her he loved her as he was punishing her. He'd never realized that his behavior had this kind of an impact on her.

Sarah, on the other hand, who rarely thinks about and almost never expresses her feelings, was silent for a very long time after she was asked what made her happy. But her parents were patient, and finally Sarah said, with a slight smile, "Ice cream makes me happy."

This was an important first step for Sarah. She wasn't yet ready to focus on other people, but she was able to talk about what aroused certain feelings in her, even anger and sadness.

This short exchange about feelings had another unexpected outcome. One day not long after their discussion, Sarah told her parents that other kids never ask her to play, and revealed that she felt "hurt." Whether she had always felt that way or this was the first time, talking about her feelings in a nonthreatening, gamelike fashion may have enabled her to recognize that tormenting and teasing others will end up hurting her, and may have contributed to her willingness to share her feelings with her parents as well.

The word "proud" was still a difficult one for Sarah to acknowledge. Although she knew what it meant ("I feel proud when I draw a good picture"), and could distinguish it from "happy," she still rarely thought about that word because she rarely felt that way. This exercise is important for Sarah because it helps her focus on good as well as not-so-good feelings. When they began exploring the word "frustrated," Sarah's father was in for a surprise. Sarah said that she was frustrated, "When Dad says 'no' all the time." Her father hadn't realized how often he must have been saying "no" to his daughter and how frustrated that made her feel.

Once children know these words and can use them in reference to themselves and others, then it's time to use ICPS to introduce some new feeling words. (With children like Sarah who are just beginning to think about feelings at all, you can continue to focus their attention on how *they* feel about things.)

"Worried" and "Relieved"

These words have special relevance to this age group, especially as a peephole into how adults feel. When Sarah's mom was explaining what made her feel worried, she said, "When you don't come home right after school and don't call home to let me know that you're all right."

Sarah was stunned. She never knew that she could worry her parents in this way, and never thought they cared. This touching anecdote perfectly illustrates my point: when parents and kids talk about how they feel in a safe atmosphere, the information they learn about each other is not only interesting but helpful. When we let children know what's on our minds, we often find out what's on theirs.

This anecdote is important in another way. It enabled Sarah to segue from thinking about her own feelings to thinking about another's. Still, she was affected by her mother's feelings about *her*. Soon, she will take that to the next level—thinking about the feelings of others that do not involve her.

"Sympathy" and "Empathy"

Although many eight- to twelve-year-olds know the meaning of the word "sympathy" (understanding another's pain), very few know the word "empathy" (feeling another's pain). Feeling empathy with others is an important part of social and emotional competence. Not only can the ability to feel another's pain inhibit someone from hurting others, it can also motivate a child to reach out and help another person in distress.

When asked what makes them feel sympathy toward someone, all three of our ICPS kids responded appropriately (e.g., "I felt sorry for Danny when he fell and broke his leg"). But only Nicholas was able to add, "I hurt inside when my friend is hurt." When asked to think about why someone might not want to hurt others, only Nicholas could say, "It would make me feel sad." Once he learned the word "empathy," which expressed what he was feeling, he enjoyed using it.

It is important to keep in mind, however, that empathy and sympathy must be kept in balance. If feeling someone's pain becomes too intense and frequent, a child may avoid that person completely to relieve himself of experiencing too much hurt.

To help our ICPS kids understand the concept of empathy, they were asked to think about more than one reason someone might want to help a child who was feeling sad to feel better. Donna said, "'Cause it would make her feel like she did good for someone." Neither her parents nor I knew whether she was experiencing that feeling deep inside, but the very fact that she was able to articulate that feeling indicated that she was well on her way. Soon Donna would be motivated to help others so she could experience their joy. This kind of empathy can propel a child to help others because it makes them feel good inside, not because they might receive material or other external rewards.

"Impatient" and "Disappointed"

A very important early warning sign of maladjustment in the adolescent years is an inability to wait and cope with the frustration of not getting what one wants. Children who can think about these words in non-anxious situations will find themselves better equipped to reduce or prevent the stresses and strains of life. Nicholas told his mother that he felt disappointed when he couldn't go skating on the pond on a rainy day, and impatient for the ice to freeze. Thinking about these feeling words helped him wait for this day to come.

Donna often waits too long, and as a result walks away empty-handed, unable to express herself. These words, however, gave her a way to think about her feelings. She said she felt "impatient" when she asks for a turn to jump rope and ends up standing around, just watching the others play. And when she doesn't get a turn, she feels "disappointed." In time, Donna would be able to tell her classmates how she feels when her wishes are unfulfilled, or even unnoticed.

Sometimes just being able to label a feeling helps us to cope. These two words would become especially meaningful for Sarah, who is still unable to identify how she feels when she can't have what she wants the minute she wants it.

Other Feeling Words: "Lonely," "Jealous," "Embarrassed"

Following the same format used above, ask your child to discuss "lonely," "jealous," and "embarrassed." Then ask your children to add feeling words of their own for you to talk about together. They'll enjoy these activities, and as in Sarah's and Donna's families, talking about how you and your child feel about things may change the way you understand each other in important ways.

Once you feel that your child has mastered these feeling words, it's time to move to two additional concepts.

Different People Can Feel Different Ways about the Same Thing

Tell your child that ICPS is going to get a little harder now, but she's ready for it. If your child enjoys gamelike activities, you can say, "We're going to play the 'Different People Can Feel Different Ways' game. Now that we have talked about what makes two people feel the same way about something, we're going to talk about how one person may feel happy about something, while another may not. First, think of something that would probably make a four-year-old feel happy that would probably *not* make a grandmother feel happy."

After her response, say, "Now think of something that might make a grandmother feel happy that would probably *not* make a four-year-old feel happy."

Follow this pattern with several combinations of people-pairs, then ask your child to come up with some pairings, including unusual or unlikely ones. Then ask, "Can you think of anything you do that makes you and (*let the child name someone*) feel different ways about the same thing?"

When Nicholas's mom asked him this question, he quickly snapped, "When I don't help with the dishes." This was interesting because not helping with the dinner dishes was a major source of contention between Nicholas and his mother, and to his sister, who didn't think he was being fair: he was angry when he did clean up the dishes, and his mother and sister were angry when he did not. Of course, the more his mother nagged, the more he resisted. Until this ICPS exercise, the situation remained at a stalemate. But as soon as Nicholas's mom asked him how he thought she felt when he ran off after dinner, something different happened.

"You feel angry, and frustrated," replied Nicholas.

Because Nicholas is now thinking about how his mother feels, and can articulate her feelings, he is more aware of the impact of his behavior on his mother and sister than if he simply experienced the ravages of their anger. He's also able to see their conflicting feelings in the context of an idea he can understand—that different people feel different ways about the same thing. This is an important component of being able to understand another's point of view.

At the same time, Nicholas's mother planted a seed for coming up with a solution to their problem. Now Nicholas knows that he will have to take both his feelings and the feelings of his mom and sister into account—not simply his own, as he had done in the past.

Sarah had difficulty responding to this activity. While she was beginning to talk about what made her feel different ways, she was still unable to simultaneously think about how what makes her feel a particular way might make another person feel.

Yet considering that Sarah rarely thought about feelings at all, including her own, her parents were pleased at the progress their daughter was making. With more time and practice, Sarah will be able to think about the more sophisticated emotions as well. It will just take time.

Donna had less difficulty joining in this game. When asked, she said that being on the Internet made her happy, but it didn't make her mother happy.

"How do you think it makes me feel when you spend too much time on the Internet?" her mother then asked.

"Worried," Donna said.

This was a breakthrough for Donna. Even though her mother had told her many times, "I worry when you spend so much time on the computer"—using the popular "I" statement so many experts advise—Donna didn't feel compelled to focus on her mother's feeling. But when Donna had to supply a feeling word directly, it riveted her attention. It was as if she experienced her mother's concern for the first time.

Feeling Different Ways about the Same Thing

Not only can different people feel different ways about the same thing, but children can now understand that one person can feel different ways about the same thing. Sometimes those feelings are successive, such as when Nicholas said, "I felt *proud* when I hit a long fly ball, but *frustrated* when the outfielder caught it."

Sarah liked thinking about this, and it helped her begin to think about others. She said, "I felt *worried* when my little brother was sick, and *relieved* when he got well." And Donna's comment—"I felt *happy* when I won first prize and then *sad* when my friend didn't"—showed genuine empathy. As one of our eight-year-olds told me, "I felt *worried* that I failed my test, and *relieved* when I got a good grade."

Not only can people feel different ways about something at different times, but children can also understand that a person can feel different ways about something at the same time. That is, they can have opposite, contradictory, or mixed emotions about something. This is the most sophisticated level of understanding about emotions. Some children, like Sarah, aren't ready for it, but more socially competent children like Nicholas can achieve it by age eight.

To try this with your child, ask, "Can you think of one thing you can feel two different ways about?"

Nicholas said that he felt disappointed and impatient when his new bike didn't come. "Okay," said his dad, "now we're going to make the question harder. Did you ever feel both good and bad about something at the same time? That's called mixed feelings."

Nicholas had to think hard about this one. Finally he said, "I feel *proud* that I got the lead in the school play, but *worried* that I won't remember my lines." This was a perfect example. Not only did Nicholas understand the concept, but by articulating his feelings he gave his parents the opportunity to help him. They could encourage him to focus on his feelings of pride in order to overcome his fears.

When Donna answered this question, she revealed something her parents never knew: "I was *happy* when I won the MVP trophy for basketball, but *nervous* that everyone came over to me to look at it." Until now, Donna's parents were not aware that anything other than joy accompanied her reaction to having received that trophy.

Most children love this exercise, possibly because of its novelty. As one ten-year-old said, "I felt *disappointed* when I was sick, but *happy* I didn't have to go to school"; and an eleven-year-old explained, "I felt *frustrated* when I broke my leg but *happy* with all the attention I got." An eight-year-old told her dad, "I was *happy* to go to summer camp, but *sad* 'cause I was homesick too." The parents of one of our twelve-year-olds found it interesting when their daughter told them, "I felt *happy* when the boy who cheats on tests got caught. He deserves it. But I also felt *sorry* for him because he was humiliated."

Games and Activities

Here are a series of games and exercises that families can use to talk about emotions. Find the ones you think will work with your family.

The TV Quiz Game

Nicholas came up with the idea for this very creative game. One night at dinner, he said, "Let's have a TV show. I'll be the host and you [meaning his parents and sister] be the contestants, and then we'll switch. I'm going to tell you something that happened to me, and the first person who knows how I felt, buzz your buzzer." Very proudly, Nicholas began. "I thought Tara stole my pencil, and accused her of it. Then I found out that she didn't. Now I feel ———. Come on, someone buzz." They all laughed and Tara said, "Embarrassed."

"One point for you," shouted Nicholas excitedly.

Index Cards

Give your children five-by-seven index cards, each with a different feeling word printed on it. Tell them to notice when something or someone makes them feel any particular way, and then to find the card and jot down on the back exactly what happened. If they can't get to this activity at the time something happens, they can focus on trying to remember the important details and write it up later.

Donna's parents knew that their daughter didn't like to talk very much. For her, the cards were a safe way to think about and express how real-life events made her feel. One day she picked the card that said "frustrated" and wrote, "The girls teased me today when I missed some baskets [in her basketball game]. But later I made a good shot and they told me how good I am and I felt *proud.*"

Cartoon Balloons

Children enjoy filling in cartoon balloons as shown in the example on page 56. Ask your child to fill in each one with a statement about what makes him feel "frustrated." Of course, your child can draw more than five balloons if he wishes. If he writes two or more things that are variations on the same theme, you can point that out and ask for something different. For example, "not winning the game" in one balloon and "not winning the race" in another are expressions of not winning. Ask, "Can you think of something different from not winning?" Children may want to draw sets of cartoon balloons for other feeling words such as "happy," "proud," "worried," and "impatient."

Your child may want to draw her own facially expressive characters underneath or over the balloons. It is not important whether the facial expressions realistically reflect the emotion being depicted. What matters is that she is interpreting the feeling word in her own way. She can fill in the balloons to reflect what she's feeling, or what she imagines someone else is feeling. This exercise is especially popular with children who, like Donna, are slow to talk about their feelings out loud.

It is easy to turn this exercise into a family activity. In gamelike fashion, siblings can play together, comparing notes about what they wrote to see if any descriptions are the same. Nicholas and

Frustrated

Tara discovered they put down several of the same things that made them feel the way described, and doing this helped them get to know each other's thoughts and feelings better. Though Sarah's brother was only four, too young to read and write, he was able to look at the pictures Sarah drew. Sarah would say the words out loud, and her brother told her what made him feel "happy," "sad," "scared," and "angry"—words he could understand. Sarah enjoyed hearing what her brother had to say. This was a wonderful way for her to recognize that her brother often felt differently than she did about things. And in playing this game with her little brother, she remembered the earlier exercise her parents introduced to her, when she thought about the "What Makes People Feel Different Ways" game. She came to realize, for example, that she feels happy when she stays on the computer, but her brother feels angry " 'cause he wants to play his games."

But it's also a perfect activity for children to do entirely by themselves, as Sarah often chose to do. She enjoyed filling in the balloons in the privacy of her own room. She was thinking about her feelings and those of others in a way she never had before.

Donna enjoyed this exercise because she could write down her thoughts without having to verbalize them.

The Feelings Story

To play this game, children make up stories using as many of the feeling words as they can. Some families enjoy creating a story together, out loud, in the form of the party game "Continuation." One person starts the story and after a few sentences says, "Continuation." The next person adds some ideas, and the game continues until the last person finishes the story.

Children who enjoy or prefer to write stories can create them on their own. Sarah's and Donna's parents, for example, give their daughters the beginnings of stories, and then the girls write down what happens next. Here's a story that Donna wrote after her parents suggested that she begin with this opening: "Two kids are playing a game together."

> Me and Tammy were playing checkers and Tammy won and I was *frustrated*. Then I was very *disappointed* because I lost the game and so I asked her to play another game and I was *proud* because I won. Another girl came over in the middle of the game and I was *worried* she'd butt in 'cause she's always buttin' in. And I was *scared* of her too. But the teacher made her go away and I was *relieved* that she wouldn't butt in. Then I was *sad* because recess was over. I asked her if I could play with her after school, and she said yes. When I went to her house I fell on the stairs and I was *embarrassed* 'cause so many people saw me fall down. So I got up and ran into her house and I was *relieved* that no one could see me.

Donna was so proud of her story that she asked if she could read it out loud at dinnertime. That was a very important first step for her: she overcame her fear of letting others know what she was feeling.

You may notice that Donna's story, though fictitious, was about *her* feelings, with no mention of anyone else's. She's aware of but still fearful of how other people feel. In the next chapter, we'll see how Donna began to overcome this fear and include the feelings of others as well as her own.

Using the Feeling Words in Real Life

Once your family is comfortable using the feeling words, and your child understands the various ways that emotions can affect people, it's time to begin applying the games and exercises I've described to real life. Rather than beginning with conflicts or problems, however, begin with a positive situation, such as when your child does well on a school project, or gets a part in the school play. The first step is to focus only on how your child feels before asking her to think about how others might feel.

Whenever the situation arises, simply ask, "How did you feel when ———?"

Once you start looking for naturally occurring opportunities to ask about feelings, you'll find many.

Nicholas's parents asked him how he felt when he figured out an answer to a computer game. He beamed, and said, "Proud." On the other hand, if he didn't do so well in his soccer game, he had no trouble sharing that he felt "frustrated."

When he started to nag his mother about when he was going to get his new computer game, she asked him, "How do you feel about having to wait until your birthday?" and he replied, "Impatient."

"Your birthday is next month," she told him. "How do you think you'll feel when it finally arrives?"

"Happy," he said. After this conversation, he stopped nagging his mom about the gift. Focusing on his happiness helped him cope with his impatience.

Another day, Nicholas was furious with his sister, who had stepped on his model plane and broken it. Because the plane was so valuable to him, he had uncharacteristic trouble controlling his anger. Sizing up the situation, Nicholas's dad waited until he thought Nicholas could talk about it, and then said, "Why don't you tell your sister how you feel about this." This suggestion (not a genuine question) was met with, "I don't want to. I might smash her head."

"Do you feel like hurting your sister over this?" his dad asked.

"Yes!" Nicholas answered.

"How would you feel if you hurt her?"

"Good! I'm really mad."

"Would you have any other feelings if you hurt Tara?"

Nicholas paused. He was still very angry, but he said, "I guess I'd feel sad if I really hurt her." Then he remembered his new word, and said, "I'd feel *empathy* too."

What a valuable, important conversation. Not only did it prevent Nicholas from committing a hurtful act for which he'd feel enormous guilt and concern—as eleven-year-old Tim did after he twisted his sister's arm in anger—but it also set the stage for him to think about what he'd do when he felt these feelings at other times. This awareness will guide him through all the later stages of problem solving.

While Sarah was able to write about feelings in non-anxious or in hypothetical situations (she loved the Cartoon Balloons), her feelings of anger and frustration shielded any thoughts about happiness and pride, and she was still unwilling to talk about her feelings at the moment that real-life conflicts arose. After a while, her parents made it easier for her to respond by simply naming several feeling words from which she could choose, including obvious, even silly choices. One day, her father asked her, "How did you feel when your friend hit you at school today—proud, relieved, or angry?" Sarah laughed, but this was an important moment—a change in the way she and her parents talked to each other.

Sarah wasn't the only one having difficulty: her parents were also occasionally uncomfortable talking about feelings. This fact, in addition to Sarah's frequent obstinacy, made them feel exasperated, and as a result they often resorted to the Power style of discipline.

Sarah was failing at school because she doodled or talked to her neighbor instead of listening to her teacher. I asked Sarah's mother how she reacted when Sarah would come home with a note from her teacher detailing a less than successful day at school. Her mother said, "I ground her and I make her do her homework"—the Power Approach in action.

"Then what happens?" I asked.

"She says she doesn't have any homework, and goes into her room and slams the door." That's when emotions would start to escalate out of control.

Sarah, her mom, and I sat down together to talk about this. First, Sarah and I talked to each other about things she likes to do. I learned she likes to draw. I asked her to draw what she does when she's not listening to her teacher. Smiling all the while, she not only drew herself talking to the child in the next seat, but also drew her teacher with a very angry face.

Next I asked her to tell me something that makes her feel *proud*, which she talked about in earlier exercises with her parents, and she said, "When I twirl on ice skates."

Then I asked her to tell me what makes her feel *frustrated*. Having just paid special attention to that word recently, she said with a knowing smile, "When Mom won't let me watch TV."

Then I asked, "How do you feel when you fail your tests at school?"

"F-R-R-R-U-S-T-E-R-A-T-E-D," she replied, playing with a word she came to love using.

"And how would you feel if you passed your tests?"

"P-R-R-O-U-D," she said with equal enthusiasm.

I then asked, "What can you do so you will feel proud?"

"Listen to the teacher."

"And how do you think your teacher would feel if you did that?"

"Proud."

The next day her mother called me, bursting with joy, and said, "Guess what Sarah told her teacher today: 'I'm going to make you proud and not frustrated.'"

Did two words, proud and frustrated—which Sarah might have had in her vocabulary but rarely, if ever, thought about— begin to turn this child around?

For Donna, our withdrawn child, it would still be a while

before she could or would verbalize these words outside of a game situation. Aware of people's feelings—including her own—she did let her parents know when she felt happy or proud about something, but it took a little longer for her to reveal negative feelings of sadness, anger, frustration, and disappointment.

Other Mini-Dialogues
with Feeling Words

You can now engage in the first stage of ICPS dialogues using the Problem-Solving Approach. To begin with, just concentrate on people's emotions. As mentioned earlier, by focusing on one part of the dialoguing process at a time, it will be easier to adjust to using this approach. If, for example, your son yells at his younger sister, you can ask:

"How do you feel when you yell at your sister?"

If your child says "Good," you can ask, "Did you also feel any different way?"

Your child may not respond to this question at first, but you are planting an important seed, alerting him to the fact that he can have several conflicting feelings at once.

You can then ask, "How might your sister feel about this?"

After your child answers, ask, "And how else might she feel?"

For now, you can conclude the dialogue with the question, "Can you think of a different way to tell your sister how you feel?"

By using this dialogue, you are encouraging sensitivity toward your son's own feelings as well as those of his sister. This will form the foundation of his ability to handle whatever frustration his sister causes for him, and to resolve the conflict peacefully.

Summing Up

- Talk to your sons as well as your daughters about feelings even if they appear to shut down. Let your sons as well as your daughters know you are there for them if they want to talk about things. Do not distance yourself emotionally from your sons even if they feel a need to be independent and convey an air of "macho" behavior.

- Ask your children to tell you how *they* feel about something instead of your telling them how you think they feel.

- Ask your children to tell you how they think their brother or sister or a friend might feel about something.

- Ask your children to tell you how they think *you* feel about something.

- When your children talk about how they feel about what happened during a conflict, ask them to think about whether the other person feels the same way or a different way about it.

- To help your children cope with the frustrations and disappointments in life, guide them to think about how they feel now, and how they might feel later.

- Guide your children to think about possible "mixed" emotions by asking them to think about whether they have opposite feelings about something at the same time. Focus on the positive side of the ledger to help relieve anxieties or other emotional stress.

- Guide your children to think about whether another person might be feeling mixed emotions about something.

- Talk about positive as well as negative emotions with your children.

Remember:

- Emotional closeness does not exclude growth of independence—it helps make your child feel he is asserting his independence within safe boundaries.

Now, let's turn our attention to another prerequisite for problem solvers: the ability to listen.

◀ 4 ▶

Is Anybody Listening?

If you think, "My child never listens to me," does your child think, "No one ever listens to me"?

Jane and Leann, coworkers at an insurance company, meet each other in the hallway. "We have to work on our outline for our presentation at the staff meeting next Tuesday," Jane says. "Let's make a time to get together. Would next Thursday at three be good for you?"

Leann, paying no attention, says, "Did you hear about the new telephone policy? I couldn't believe it!"

Leann hadn't heard a word Jane said.

We've all been in situations like this. Sometimes, like Jane, we realize that our message fell on deaf ears. How do you feel when this happens to you?

Other times, like Leann, we walk away from a conversation unable to recall a single word the other person said. Because we were so focused on what we wanted to say, we spent the entire time waiting for an opening. How do you feel when you walk away from a conversation like this?

Now think about conversations you have with your children. How many times do you ask them if they're listening to you?

Do you ever stop to wonder if you listen—really listen—to them?

We tend to take listening for granted. Yet many of us, adults and kids alike, don't listen well. As a result, we can't problem solve. If we don't really listen to what people say to us, or what we say to others, we don't know what's at issue, and what to do.

Take the case of Jane and Leann. Leann meant no disrespect; she had something else on her mind and couldn't put it aside. As a result, both women ended up talking to themselves rather than to each other. This happens in families too. We respond to statements we think we hear, and say things that are never heard. We make erroneous assumptions about how other people are feeling and what they are thinking, and some problems never get resolved. The inability to listen well is at the root of many conflicts. It's important for everyone to listen and pay attention— spouses to each other, and children and parents to each other as well. No one likes not feeling heard.

The ability to listen is the third core component of the ability to problem solve. When we learn to be good listeners and really pay attention, we:

- Respect the other person, showing that we care about what he or she has to say
- Avoid drawing faulty conclusions about the other person's thoughts and feelings, which helps us to avert potential conflicts
- Learn if the other person has thoughts and feelings about things that may be different from ours, which is a prerequisite for problem solving
- Notice important cues that help us understand what the other person is thinking and feeling

There are many reasons we don't always listen. Sometimes we're too preoccupied with our own feelings and thoughts to pay attention. Other times, we tune out—choose not to listen—because we're simply not interested, or because we're angry. Few things are more exasperating for parents than a child who appears to be listening but isn't. If you think that your child is tuning you out on a regular basis, there may be several reasons why she's doing so:

- She has become immune to the Power Approach and no longer fears being punished
- You're giving her Suggestions she's already thought of
- You're giving her Explanations she's already heard, or already knows

Fortunately, one of the biggest advantages of the Problem-Solving Approach is that children listen because they're participating in the conversation. And just as important, you will find yourself listening more to what your child has to say.

But before launching into actual ICPS dialogues, we have to hone our listening skills and those of our kids. Here are some tips that will help even the most tuned-out kid to listen, while at the same time improve the listening skills of even the best listener.

Teaching Children to Listen

One of the best ways to raise children who are good listeners is to model good listening skills. When parents really listen to each other, not only will the relationship improve, but they'll show their children the value and importance of paying attention.

There are also several games that can teach children to listen. Here's one that eight- to twelve-year-olds love to practice. It's called "Silly Skits."

The idea is to demonstrate, in exaggerated fashion, how outrageous it sounds when someone isn't listening. You can begin with the skits I've included below, having two children, or a parent and child, read alternate lines.

To begin, say to your child:

We're going to read some Silly Skits. Listen to this conversation. There's something silly about the way these two people talk to each other. At the end of this skit, tell me why you think it is funny.

A: I got a racing car for Christmas.

B: I don't like blueberries.

A: My racing car is the fastest on the block.

B: My mom made me eat blueberry pie last night.

A: It's red and has a white top.

B: I feel sick today.

A: I got other things too.

B: I'd rather have chocolate cake.

A: I got a new shirt too.

B: My mom says that's not good for my teeth.

A: Why not?

B: I'll get cavities and get fat.

A: How could a new shirt make you get cavities and fat?

After your child says, "These two characters aren't listening to each other," ask your child:

"Are they listening to each other, or to themselves?"

When your child answers, say, "Now let's read this skit again. There is one place where A *does* listen to B. When you hear it, let me know by raising your hand" (or tapping your knee—whatever your child chooses to do).

When your child correctly identifies the moment of real listening, suggest a new addition to the game. This time, ask your child to come up with a response that would show that the person was really listening. For example:

A: "I got a racing car for Christmas."

Now ask, "What could B say or ask that would show he/she heard what A said?"

B: ———.

After B answers, say, "Now make up the rest of the skit so it isn't silly, because each character is listening to the other."

Here's another Silly Skit you can present to your child. This time tell him to listen carefully for the time when B is listening to A, and when he hears it, to raise his hand.

A: I feel frustrated today.
B: I got new shoes for my birthday.
A: I've blown up five balloons, and they all popped.
B: My shoes are white with brown tips.
A: I have two blue balloons and three yellow balloons.
B: I wish my shoes were red with pink tips.
A: I wish I could blow them up without popping them.
B: That's hard to do.
A: I know. You have to be careful.
B: How can you blow up shoes, anyway?

Once your child identifies the moment correctly, ask him to make up a skit that is not silly. Start again with the first line:

A: I feel frustrated today.

After this, encourage children to make up their own Silly Skits. I've found that children enjoy this kind of activity: it taps in to their own creativity. One child can create a skit on his own and read it to the entire family, or children can collaborate and create a skit together, each taking a part. Suggest that the skit contain some lines that indicate that the two characters are listening to each other, and instruct them to put an "X" next to those lines.

Here is a skit that Nicholas playfully created:

> *A*: I lost my pencil.
> *B*: I cooked hamburgers and they burned.
> *A*: Do you have another pencil?
> *B*: My mom will be mad 'cause I ruined the hamburgers.
> *A*: I can't seem to find my pencil anywhere.
> *B*: Do you know how to cook?
> *A*: I can't do my homework without my pencil.
> X *B*: Do you want one of my pencils?
> *A*: Yes, I know how to cook.
> *B*: I will get you one of my pencils.
> X *A*: Thank you.

This is a good example of Nicholas's ability to play this game, creating two people preoccupied with their own needs. His family particularly enjoyed listening for the lines which Nicholas had marked with an X.

Next, Nicholas and his sister, Tara, rewrote this skit to reflect good listening.

> *A*: I lost my pencil.
> *B*: Here, you can use mine.
> *A*: Thanks.
> *B*: I burned my hamburgers.
> *A*: Why?
> *B*: I cooked them too long. Mom will be mad.
> *A*: Tell her you're sorry.
> *B*: Okay.

How do other children react to Silly Skits? Sarah loved them. She laughed out loud while reading parts with her mother. Though she couldn't generate one of her own, because she was still slow to express her thoughts and feelings to others, she understood what was going on.

Donna, interestingly, wrote a skit that included someone's feelings.

    A: Rufus (the dog) ran away today.
    B: My bird said hello.
    A: I love Rufus.
    B: I taught my bird to talk.
    A: I'm scared he'll die.
X *B*: I'll buy you a new dog.
X *A*: Thanks.

After your children are familiar with this activity, ask them, "Why do you think we made up Silly Skits? What do we learn from them?"

If your child can put her finger on the answer, then it's time to start using the Silly Skits in real life. The next time your child does not appear to be listening to you, or to his brother or sister, simply ask, "Do you remember the Silly Skits? Are you listening to me?"

Sarah's mom found an ingenious way to incorporate Silly Skits into daily life. If she sensed that Sarah wasn't listening, she simply said, "I got a racing car for Christmas." This was her shorthand way of gently and humorously reminding Sarah of the need to listen. And Sarah always smiled.

Sarah also began to understand that other people are bothered when she doesn't listen to them as well. A few days later, Sarah told her mom, "Sometimes I don't listen to what the kids want to do. Barbie told me I only care about myself." Before ICPS, Sarah might not have cared about that.

When asked whether her friends minded that she sometimes didn't listen to them, another ICPS girl, aged ten, had an important insight: "My friend was singing a song and I wasn't listening. She said I hurt her feelings." And then she added, "I guess I should listen to my teacher too, so I'll do better in school."

Why Listen?

As I mentioned earlier, listening to others is a way of respecting them. But there are other important reasons to listen, which have a direct impact on how well we problem solve.

Avoiding False Conclusions

Sometimes not listening and not paying close attention can result in hearing only part of what people say, leading to faulty conclusions and conflicts that could have been avoided.

Let's take the case of two fourth-graders. Lisa wants Maria to stop teasing her, so she says, "You can't come to my party if you keep teasing me." But Maria only heard, "You can't come to my party." As a result, she feels rejected. Lisa didn't intend to reject Maria; she wanted Maria to stop her teasing. So Maria feels bad for nothing. At the same time, because she didn't listen, she never addressed the second, more important part of Lisa's statement—that she needs to stop teasing Lisa. So the conflict is perpetuated rather than solved, all because of faulty listening.

The popular party game "Telephone" is a fun way to help children focus on the importance of hearing the *whole* message.

One person starts a message by whispering it very quickly in another person's ear. The second person whispers the message he heard into a third person's ear until everyone present is given a whispered message. Then, the last person says aloud what he was told—which is almost always a preposterously mangled version of the original statement.

Families enjoy playing "Telephone" together, making up their own messages. Or you can try some of these:

- I don't like to run when I'm tired 'cause I might bump into a tree and fly to the ground and lose the race.
- I flew to Las Vegas and I wasn't in a plane 'cause I flew with my arms and won a thousand dollars in two days.
- I eat sunflower seeds and pickles and I fly in the sky at night and I don't like to sleep except during the day.

Next, you can expand this game by focusing on the question *Did you get the whole message?*

Present the family with the playlet below. Anyone in the family can read the parts, as Donna did with her father, or you can use puppets.

Donna: Sammy's a scaredy cat.
Father: What did he say?
Donna: He's scared of flies.
Father: Did you get the whole message?
Donna: I guess so.
Father: Why don't you ask him again to make sure you got the whole message.
(*Donna walks away, pretending to go to school.*)
Donna (*long pause*): I went to school and talked to Sammy. He said he's not scared of flies.
Father: What is he scared of?
Donna: He said he's scared to *kill* flies.
Father: Oh, so the first time, you only heard part of the message.
Donna: Yeah.

As soon as they finished reading the playlet, Donna's father asked her some questions about it:

What was Sammy's whole message?
What part of the message did you not hear?
What did you learn from reading this playlet?
Why is it important to listen to what other people say?

Getting the Whole Message
in Real Life

One day Donna came home and told her parents, "Jodie doesn't like me." Her father asked her how she knew that, and Donna said, "She told me."

Her father then asked, "Do you remember the playlet we read about getting the whole message?"

"Yeah," replied Donna.

"Are you sure you got the whole message?" asked her dad.

"Yeah," answered Donna.

Her father then asked, "How can you find out if you got the whole message?"

"I could ask her?" answered Donna. The next day Donna came rushing home with excitement, announcing, "Jodie likes me."

"What happened?" asked her dad.

"She said she doesn't like me when I lie to her."

Donna's father then took this opportunity to engage her in an important dialogue:

Father: What did you learn from this?
Donna: To get the whole message.
Father: Yes, to listen. How did you feel before you got the
    whole message?
Donna: Sad . . . and worried.

Father: How do you feel now?
Donna: Happy . . . and relieved. And I'm not going to lie
   to her anymore.

Other children thought about this too, when I asked them,
"Can you think of a time when you heard part of the message,
not the whole message, so you got the wrong message?"

I *heard* Tommy (my brother) say he was going to beat me
   up.
The whole message: . . . if I don't stop taking his bike.

I *heard* Louisa threaten to tell all the kids about the mole
   on my back.
The whole message: . . . if I lie to her one more time.

Understanding What People Want

Another reason it is important to listen to others is that it helps
us understand what they're thinking and feeling. This way, we
come to realize that others may think and feel differently than we
do about the same thing.

Here is an exercise that families can engage in at the dinner
table, in the car, or any time everyone is together. Nicholas and
his family started this way:

Mother: I'm going to tell you five things I like and five things I
don't like. Listen carefully, because you have to remember them.
   I like:

- Hamburgers
- Mystery novels
- The color blue
- Crossword puzzles
- When Nicholas cleans his room

I don't like:

- When Nicholas and Tara fight
- Nicholas's messy room
- The color orange
- To argue with my kids
- Heavy-metal rock music

Nicholas named most of what his mom said, Tara remembered a few more, and Dad finished it off. Then it was Nicholas's and Tara's turn to name things they liked and didn't like, an activity they relished. Dad, too, had a turn.

After everyone was finished, Nicholas's mom asked, "Why did we play this game? What do you have to do to be good at it?"

"Listen," chanted Nicholas.

"Pay attention," answered Tara.

"Did we learn anything about each other that we didn't know before?" Mom asked.

Tara said she never knew her mom liked crossword puzzles.

"How can knowing things about people help us solve problems with each other?" Mom asked.

Nicholas knew. "I'll try not to mess up my room," he said.

And Dad was careful not to buy his wife an orange blouse for a birthday present even though it had caught his eye.

Sarah liked this game and when it was her turn to name what she liked, she said, "I would like to learn to play the drums"— something her parents never knew.

Delighted, they were eager to buy her a drum set, though first they spoke with her about good times to practice so as not to bother anybody. Sarah quickly found herself very involved in and excited about her new hobby. This simple memory game was a turning point for Sarah and her family.

Even Donna, who still didn't like to talk much, found a way to participate in this activity. After her mother named five things she liked and five things she didn't like, Donna wrote down those items she could remember, and gave the list to her mother. Donna was proud of herself for being able to do that—and with reason. Donna had to listen and pay careful attention to remember the items on her mother's list.

A more challenging version of this game is to combine it with use of feeling words from Chapter 3. One person can name five different feelings, and give the others one example that brings out each of those five different feelings. The others have to remember both the feeling and what was said about that feeling. Nicholas's and Tara's mother started this game by saying:

> I feel *happy* when we eat out.
> I feel *worried* when Nicholas isn't home for dinner on time.
> I feel *angry* when Nicholas and Tara fight.
> I feel *frustrated* when no one listens to me.
> I feel *empathy* when someone gets hurt.

Each person in the family can choose his or her own feeling words, and the number of different words can be decided by the ability and interest level of the children involved in the game. To make this even more challenging, see if someone can remember what Mom said after others have had their turns. A still more demanding version is to ask everybody to name something about which he or she has mixed emotions, as described in Chapter 3.

By playing this game, Nicholas learned that his sister was happy when she saw a scary movie. If she had ever told him that before, he never heard it.

Noticing Important Cues

Finally, when children learn to listen well, they also learn to pay attention to important cues that give them an idea of how other people feel. These cues can involve facial expressions, body language, tone of voice, or even what people actually say.

For example, if I'm enjoying loud rock music and a friend enters the room frowning, do I notice her facial expression or am I too preoccupied? If she quickly walks out of the room, what conclusion do I draw: that she doesn't like the music or that she has somewhere else to go? Or do I not think about her expression at all? If she bluntly tells me the music is too loud, do I even hear her?

To help children learn to pay attention to visual and verbal cues, especially those which signal that a person feels different ways about the same thing, you can play the "How Can This Be?" game. Say to your child:

> Sally was chosen for the lead in the class play. She feels very happy and proud. Andrea got chosen for the lead in her school play. She feels anxious and worried. How could this be?

If you have two or more children, each can give a reason for each scenario. If you have one child, you can offer one reason, then let your child give a different one.

After you generate several possibilities, ask:

> How could you tell by looking how Sally feels about that?
> How could you tell by looking how Andrea feels about that?
> How could you tell by listening to what Sally says?
> How could you tell by listening to what Andrea says?

Here are some other scenarios you can try:

> A ten-year-old and her mother feel different ways when her room is messy.

How might the ten-year-old feel?
How might her mom feel?
How could you tell by looking how the ten-year-old (or
the mom) feels about that?
How could you tell by listening to the ten-year-old (or the
mom)?

Frank and Derrick both went on a roller-coaster ride.
They each felt a different way about this.
How might each child have felt?
How could you tell?

Now let your children make up some scenarios of their own. This game is harder than it sounds, because often children respond by describing how children feel about different experiences. When Donna was asked how JoAnne and Jeannie felt about playing in the snow, she said, "JoAnne's happy because she's playing in the snow," and "Jeannie's sad because she's on punishment and can't go out and play in the snow."

But at issue is the question of how JoAnne and Jeannie could feel different ways about the *same* thing, in this case playing in the snow. To focus Donna's attention on this question, her mom had to ask, "Could JoAnne and Jeannie feel different ways about playing in the snow?" When Donna still didn't understand, her mom asked, "How does JoAnne feel about playing in the snow?"

Then Donna said, "Happy, because she's making snowballs."

Her mom then said, "Make up a reason that Jeannie could feel a different way about playing in the snow."

"She's frustrated," Donna said, "'cause she keeps falling." That's when she understood how Jeannie and JoAnne could have different feelings about the same activity.

Even Nicholas had trouble with this at first. The example he created featured Tommy, who felt happy because he made the football team, and Troy, who was jealous because he didn't make the team. To help him understand the concept, his mom had to ask him, "Could two boys feel different ways about being on the football team?"

"Yeah, one could feel proud that he was picked, and one could feel scared of getting hurt," Nicholas said.

Encouraging children to think of how different people can feel different ways about the same thing by noticing their facial expressions, body language, and other cues can help them listen and pay attention to important cues in real life.

In Real Life

Part of the reason Nicholas was able to make friends and keep friends is because he's a good listener. Instead of flying off the handle when his friend called at the last minute to tell him he couldn't go to the movies, as I described in Chapter 1, Nicholas heard his explanation (that he was sick), and responded to his friend's needs.

In contrast, consider what happened when Sarah wanted to play kick ball with Carla, another girl at school. Carla refused— but Sarah was so consumed with her desire to play that she didn't even hear the refusal. Nor did she notice that when she asked to play kick ball, Carla slumped her shoulders and turned her head away, expressionless. Had Sarah listened and paid attention to the disinterested cues that Carla expressed, she might have recognized that Carla felt a different way than she did about playing kick ball, and might have been able to find out what she did want to do. Instead, Sarah was so focused on her own desires that she couldn't do anything but plead with Carla. In the end, she stormed away, angry. The two children never did play together.

As part of one ICPS exercise, parents ask their children to think about whether they ever learn something about someone just by looking at him or her. One twelve-year-old girl said, "A new kid at school was mean. I could tell 'cause she kept bumping into people and knocking them out of the way." Another girl was happy that she noticed that her friend looked sad. She told her dad, "I asked her what was wrong and she said her bird died, and I made her feel better."

Donna, though socially withdrawn, was sensitive to verbal and nonverbal cues, but didn't know what to do about the information they gave her. She reacted to them by walking away, often pouting. Because she was not adept at thinking of alternative solutions or sequenced planning, the two problem-solving skills her parents were yet to teach her, Donna found it safest to simply avoid difficult people and sidestep problems she couldn't solve. Children like Donna don't need as much help with this skill as children like Sarah, but need to learn the other skills so they can put their sensitivity to cues to good use—skills both Donna and Sarah will learn in Chapters 6, 7, and 8.

Using the Problem-Solving Approach: ICPS Dialogues in Real Life

Now it's time to take all these newly honed listening skills and put them to use in ICPS dialogues.

Suppose your son wants to play chess with his sister, but is rebuffed. You can say to your son:

- How do you feel when your sister won't play chess with you?
- How do you think your sister feels when you call her names because you're angry?

After your child replies, say: "You want to play chess but your sister doesn't. What does your sister like to do? Can you think of a way to use that information now?"

It is important for your son to distinguish between his sister's not wanting to play chess because of lack of interest, or because she just doesn't want to play chess at that time. If the latter, your son can find out what his sister would rather do. If she doesn't want to do anything, then your son needs to know this, and find a way to respect it. By listening and paying attention, and learning not to focus only on his own preoccupations and wants, your child has taken an important step toward eventual resolution of this conflict.

Now let's see how focusing on listening skills helps Sarah. She complained that children didn't want to play with her and that they didn't like her. In the past, Sarah's mother would have tried grounding her when she heard that Sarah had been acting like a bully (Power), or telling her to treat the kids at school with kindness (Suggestions), or even explaining that she doesn't have friends because she makes them afraid of her (Explanations). But this time, Sarah's mom began to dialogue with the Problem-Solving Approach by asking her daughter: "How do you think someone feels when you tease them?"

When Sarah's mom first began asking this question, Sarah would say, "I feel good." This is typical of aggressive children. However, Sarah's mother persevered. She kept asking the same question whenever it came up, and this time, Sarah gave a more appropriate response: "They feel bad."

Next Sarah's mother asked:

How can you tell they're feeling this way?
What can you notice by looking at them?
What can you notice by listening to them?
How do you really feel when you do that?
If you want someone to play with you, how can you find out what they might like to do?

In response to the last question, Sarah said, "Listen and pay attention." What a wonderful response! Sarah and her mother had never had a conversation like this before.

Not only was Sarah learning to listen, and think about what she was doing, but her mother was listening more to what Sarah had to say. Instead of being preoccupied by Sarah's misbehavior, and subsequently imposing punishments, she heard how her child feels, perhaps for the first time.

Sarah didn't react by slamming her bedroom door when she felt angry about her lack of friends. Instead, she was able to articulate to her mom that the other kids are mad at her, and that she teases them because she's mad too. She's still not capable of empathy. And she wasn't able to ask one of her classmates what she'd like to do instead, or even to observe what they were doing when she asked to play. But she was starting to respond to the skills her parents have been working on with her. She was starting to pay attention to the fact that her mother cared about how she felt. With more practice, Sarah would soon care how she felt too.

This was an important beginning.

Summarizing Tips

- When your children respond with a statement that has nothing to do with what you or another person said, remind them of the "Silly Skits." That often redirects the conversation and puts it back on course.

  Note: If your child is preoccupied with something that's deeply bothering her, take her aside and help her through it by talking about her feelings as discussed in Chapter 3.

- When your children are bothered by something someone has said (e.g., "Jodie doesn't like me"), ask, "How do you know that? Did you get the whole message?" Encourage them to find out if they got the whole message.

- If you and your child are in conflict over a specific issue, ask: "Can you and I feel a different way about the same thing? When you leave your clothes on the floor, how do you feel about that? How do you think I feel about that? How can you tell?" If necessary, give your child hints, such as, "Look at my face," or "What tone of voice am I using?" You can use the same approach if your child is in conflict with a sibling or another child.

- If your children are tuning out when you talk to them, ask yourself if you are telling them what they already know, or if you are letting them express what they're thinking and feeling. Ask them to tell you how they feel, how they think you (or the person involved) feels, and, when appropriate (e.g., if they say, "No one will play with me"), ask whether finding out more about another person's preferences and interests would help solve the problem at hand.

- If you carefully tune in to your children's facial expressions and body language when they first seem uncomfortable, you can begin the ICPS dialogue and keep the situation from escalating out of control. Be especially sensitive to changes in posture and facial expressions in your son, who may, more so than your daughter, be acting cheerful and strong on the outside while hiding feelings of sadness on the inside.

- If you genuinely listen to your children, they will listen to you too.

◀ 5 ▶

Are Things Always
What They Seem to Be?

Just as we can stretch our bodies for greater flexibility,
we can stretch our minds for greater possibilities.

In the last chapter, I showed that if we don't listen well, we may end up feeling angry at someone for the wrong reason. In the same vein, not thinking through why people do what they do can also cause misunderstandings and problems. More often than we realize, people do and say things for reasons that are completely different than the reasons we assume. Things are not always as they seem to be.

I once felt very worried that a colleague was going to turn down an important request because she didn't call when she said she would. I could have saved myself considerable anxiety had I taken the time to find out *why* she didn't call. As I later learned, she had to leave town suddenly to tend to a family emergency, and forgot all of her immediate obligations at work. Her failure to call was forgetful at best and thoughtless at worst; however, in no way was she relaying the message to me that I thought she was. Not only was she not turning down my request, she wasn't thinking of me at all!

When people draw hasty, inaccurate conclusions about another's motivation, they can misinterpret that person's intent.

From working with families, I've realized that sometimes people fail to gather all the facts in the moment, and sometimes the failure occurs over time.

Let me explain. If Will lends a basketball to Charles and Charles doesn't return it, Will can assume that Charles is thoughtless, or that he's selfish and wants to keep it, or he may assume that Charles lost it and is afraid to say so. In all of these cases, Will is considering Charles's failure to return the ball in light of what's happening *at a given moment*.

Suppose, though, that Andrea is angry at her friend Monique because Monique brags about her looks. Andrea can assume that Monique likes to brag (a superficial motive), or, if she has a deeper level of insight, she may realize that deep down Monique feels weak and insecure. In both cases, she's considering Monique's *habitual behavior over time*.

Both of these dimensions of understanding—how well we consider another's actions in the moment or over time—affect how we navigate our way through our interpersonal worlds.

Momentary Exchanges: "Why Did He Do That?"

Children, like adults, often work themselves up into emotional turmoil when they don't have enough information at hand during a momentary exchange. If I pass a girl on the street and she doesn't wave at me, I can assume she doesn't like me—without thinking that possibly she didn't see me, or was preoccupied and didn't mean to snub me. Peter Goldenthal, in his book *Beyond Sibling Rivalry*, describes how easily comments can be misinterpreted as teasing when they may not have been meant that way at all.

Other times, motives are misunderstood because we aren't sensitive to the visual cues the other person is relaying. If I were to notice, for example, that the girl who passes me in the street without waving is walking very fast, I can consider the possibility that the reason she didn't wave was because she was in such a rush, and perhaps she didn't see me at all.

Gathering Enough Information

To sensitize children to the possibility that there is more than one reason people do what they do, suggest that the family play the "Why Else" game using hypothetical characters.

At the dinner table or whenever the family is together, parents can begin by saying, "I'm going to tell you about a situation involving a girl named Betsy, and you try to think of as many reasons as you can that would explain why Betsy acts the way she does. For example, Betsy didn't play with her friend today because . . ."

When Donna was asked this question, she said:

Betsy was tired.
She [Betsy] thought her friend didn't like her anymore.
She had to do her homework.
She had to go to the doctor.
She doesn't like her anymore.

Not only did Donna come up with a variety of reasons, but she was now beginning to say them out loud and with some enthusiasm.

Sarah focused primarily on negative reasons:

Betsy doesn't want to be her friend.
She doesn't like her.

Although we saw in Chapter 3 that Sarah was beginning to recognize how other people feel, she was still unable to imagine that anyone would act differently than she would.

After letting children come up with several answers, focus your instructions so that they reflect the character's motivations. "Let's suppose that Ben walks right by Donald without saying hello. Think of at least one reason why Ben would do this without meaning to hurt Donald's feelings."

Nicholas said:

He didn't see him.

He had to hurry because his mother told him to come right home after school.

He was upset 'cause his aunt died.

Other friends were rushing him to go somewhere.

Nicholas was able to think of several different possibilities without any trouble.

Sarah was beginning to like this game, and was willing to think hard. Although she came up with only one possibility— "His knee hurts and he wants to go home"—this was an important insight for her, because it was the first time she thought of a motivation that wasn't negative.

When Donna was asked why Ben walked by Donald without saying hello, she said, "He's too shy." This is a perfect example of how people tend to attribute behavior in others according to how they would act themselves. Though this was a momentary exchange, Donna interpreted Ben's behavior using deeper insight into his character, a subject we'll explore later in this chapter.

After the children name as many reasons as they can think of in this category, say: "Now think of at least one reason that Ben would act this way if he did want to hurt Donald's feelings."

Nicholas, Donna, and Sarah all answered this question easily, giving some variation of:

He doesn't like him.

He doesn't want to be his friend.

Nicholas added, "On a bet, I'll give you twenty dollars not to talk to Donald."

Here are some other scenarios parents can use:

- Rudy asks Beth if her father is going to take her to the zoo today. Beth gets upset and walks away. Maybe Beth is angry at Rudy.
  Why Else?
- Sally comes storming into the house and slams her bedroom door. Her mother thinks she's doing that to annoy her.
  Why Else?
- Marvin is not listening to the teacher today. The teacher thinks he's not interested in the lesson.
  Why Else?

Eventually, ask your child to make up her own scenarios and list all the different reasons people do the things they do.

Not only are aggressive children more likely than shy or adjusted ones to assume a negative motive when people don't do what they'd like them to, but they are also more likely to respond in negative ways. You can learn how your child might react when she's disappointed by a friend by playing the "What Did You Say Next" game using hypothetical characters.

Say to your child:

Tina and Lisa made plans to go to the movies on Saturday afternoon. On Saturday morning Tina calls and tells Lisa she is sick and can't go. Tina says she felt bad to disappoint Lisa and she waited until the morning because she hoped she'd be better and could go. What did Lisa say next?

Nicholas and Donna, both of whom felt sympathy for Tina, said that Lisa would tell Tina she's sorry she's sick, and hopes she gets well soon. Donna even offered to come to her house to see how she was doing. Sarah, on the other hand, said Lisa would be mad. When asked what she would say next, Sarah said she'd tell Tina she should have called sooner because now it's too late to find someone else to go to the movies. Sarah also assumed Tina was lying and just didn't want to go with her.

Next, ask your child to think of what Lisa could say if she did want to hurt Tina's feelings, and if she did not.

After children get into the habit of listing several possible explanations and reactions to another's behavior, parents can combine this skill with the skill of understanding people's feelings that we focused on in Chapter 3. Nicholas's parents, for instance, asked him about the scenario involving Ben and Donald.

"Let's say that Ben walks by Donald because he doesn't want to be his friend anymore. How might Donald feel if that is the reason?"

"Sad," answered Nicholas. "And worried that he lost his friend."

"Would Donald feel any differently if he thought that maybe Ben was upset 'cause his aunt died?" Nicholas's mom asked.

"Yes, he would feel sad for him."

"And what's our new big word?"

"Empathy," said Nicholas proudly.

Then Mom asked, "And how about if he just didn't see him?"

"I guess he wouldn't worry," said Nicholas.

"And if he had to hurry home?" asked Mom.

"He'd understand that too."

Even Sarah began to enjoy this exercise. Talking about other people's feelings in fictitious situations that did not involve her, and recognizing that people might do what they do for reasons other than to hurt, helped her lessen her anger.

As you help your child to understand why other people act

in certain ways, think about various reasons your children do what they do. If you have a child who bullies or teases others, for example, think about why she might be doing that. It is possible that your child may feel overpowered and has a need to regain control over her life.

Ross Greene, in describing children more explosive than Sarah, illustrates how a child who blurts out emotionally laden words may not mean to hurt another's feelings but may be expressing herself that way because she feels out of control. Children like Sarah can also spiral out of control. By making the distinction between intentional hurt and loss of control, you can decide how much to focus your child's attention on the other person's feelings, and how much to focus first on her own.

Reading Visual Cues

When children practice thinking of why people do what they do in the abstract, they train themselves to gather the information they need to draw accurate conclusions. Noticing visual cues helps them make accurate judgments as well.

In Chapter 4, I mentioned such visual cues as facial expressions and body language. These cues help us to interpret another's motivation. Some people don't notice these cues at all. Others do notice cues, but select irrelevant ones, or interpret those they do notice inaccurately. In this section, we'll focus on helping children to pay attention to visual cues and to interpret them accurately.

Sometimes the way in which we interpret another's behavior is defined by the behavior of the person doing the interpreting. Ken Dodge and his colleagues have found, for example, that aggressive boys are more likely than others to view ambiguous acts as hostile and to react in kind. But some girls react this way as well. When one of Sarah's classmates bumped into her, Sarah told me that the other child meant it. A child who isn't aggressive is more likely to consider the possibility that this act was an accident, and that the other child meant no harm. Such a child would also gather information about what led up to the act before responding.

On the other hand, aggressive children do not react with hostility if they recognize that the act is clearly not hostile. Thus, it is important that we help children like Sarah think about how to evaluate ambiguous acts—so they can determine whether the act was meant to harm, or if it was unintentional. If the act is deliberate, then Sarah needs to think about how she can react to it. If the act is not deliberate, then Sarah needs to practice not reacting to it as if it were.

Activities for Reading Visual Cues

One way to help aggressive children make this distinction and learn the necessary skills is to focus on visual cues. Present some fictitious scenarios that are ambiguous with regard to intent so as to allow for more than one interpretation. These scenarios will allow you to discuss cues about people's facial expressions and body language.

Using pictures 1a–1d, say: "I'm going to show you some pictures and then I'm going to ask you to tell a story about what is happening in them. Let's call the two girls Carla and Monique." If your child's story does *not* refer to the issues raised by them, ask:

- What did Carla do or say after Monique bumped into her?
- Why was Monique bending down?
- Did you notice anything about Monique's facial expression that would tell you what happened?

1a

1b

1c

1d

- Did you notice anything else about Monique that would tell you what happened?

Nicholas's story included several of the cues without having to be asked about them. He said, "Monique bumped into Carla because she wasn't looking where she was going and she looked worried. She offered to help pick up the books, and Carla said, 'That's okay,' and they both picked up the books."

Nicholas understood that it was an accident "because Monique looked apologetic." He also noticed that Monique started to bend down to pick up the books. Nicholas missed only one cue—Monique's putting her hand over her mouth, a gesture of embarrassment. But he did notice her facial expression, and interpreted her bending down in a positive way; that is, she wanted to clean up the mess.

Sarah, on the other hand, assumed that Monique bumped into Carla on purpose to knock the books out of her hand. When asked why she thought that, Sarah said, "Monique started to step on the books." In other words, Sarah interpreted Monique's bending down as hostile. Sarah focused on the bump instead of the cues accompanying the bump, and paid no attention to Monique's facial expression. Instead, she focused on the misinterpreted cue—bending down to step on the books. Sarah's parents need to help her become a more accurate reader of visual information.

Donna, for her part, paid attention to Monique's facial expression, but being fearful of others, interpreted it as anger instead of regret. To help Donna look at this visual cue in other ways, her dad said to her, "That's one possible way to interpret Monique's expression. Can you think of a different way?"

Now ask your child to look at picture 1e. Monique's facial expression shows anger. She's bending down with her foot slightly raised in the air; she appears to be preparing to step on the books. Return to picture 1d, in which Monique is bending down with both feet on the ground.

1e

Ask: "Do you notice anything different about Monique in this picture than in the one you saw before?"

Now that Monique's hostile intention is clear, all three children—including Sarah—noticed both Monique's facial expression and body posture.

Sarah's mother then asked her daughter to look again at picture 1d, and asked: "Is there any reason Monique might be bending down in this picture (1d) that would be different from this picture (1e)? Sarah looked carefully at both pictures—a big step in itself for her. In response to her mother's specific question, Sarah noticed that Monique looked angrier in picture 1e than in picture 1d. Because Sarah still did not spontaneously suggest that Monique's motives might be different in the two pictures, her mom asked, "Is it possible that one of these pictures shows more clearly than the other that Monique is going to step on the books?"

Sarah then pointed to picture 1e and said, "Here she just looks like she is." Her mom then asked what Monique might be doing in picture 1d. Sarah said she wasn't sure. Now that her attention was focused on the contrast between the two pictures, Sarah was at least pausing before assigning a motive to Monique in picture 1d.

Next, encourage your child to interpret the behavior of others, in terms of whether an act is hostile or accidental, using people in their own lives. Ask your child, "Has anyone ever bumped into you?" Regardless of the answer, follow with:

Why do you think that happened (or could have happened)?
Why Else?
What did you (or could you) notice about the person before jumping to conclusions?
If someone bumped into you because (reason #1), how would you probably feel?
If someone bumped into you for that reason, what might you do or say next?

If someone bumped into you because (reason #2), how would you probably feel?
If someone bumped into you for that reason, what might you do or say next?
Would finding out the reason change what you might say or do next?
Is it a good idea to find out why someone did something before getting angry?

If your child doesn't offer possibilities that could be both deliberate and unintentional, ask:

Do you think that child bumped into you by accident or on purpose?
What would you do or say next if you thought it was on purpose?
What would you do or say next if you thought it was an accident?

Nicholas and Donna both recognized that the bumping might have been accidental. If so, they both agreed that they would have said something like "That's okay." But if it were on purpose, they both said that the action could start a fight. This response is interesting, in light of the fact that in real life, starting a fight is something Nicholas probably *would* not do and Donna *could* not do.

Sarah, on the other hand, was quick to assume that the bumping was on purpose, and at first couldn't even consider any other possibilities. She did, however, notice the difference in facial expression and body posture when it was specifically pointed out to her. It's important for Sarah's parents—and eventually for Sarah—to create more scenarios with multiple possibilities so that she can draw on these lessons when thinking about what happens in real life.

Sarah's parents wanted her to pay more attention to how things people do can make others feel. They introduced one more situation—a girl broke something of value to another girl. Next they asked Sarah to come up with reasons why the first girl would break something if she wanted to hurt the other girl. Sarah said, "She wanted revenge. That kid broke something of hers," and then added, "or she wouldn't let her use it." When asked to come up with reasons that would not hurt the other girl's feelings, Sarah replied, "She dropped it but she didn't mean to," and, "She was running and didn't see it." Although all children enjoy this exercise, it is especially important for children who are aggressive, either physically or verbally.

One way to encourage children to create their own scenarios which they can then evaluate in terms of intent is to ask them to draw a situation themselves. They can draw characters (even stick figures will do) that tell a story, and caption their drawing. You can get them started by asking the following questions:

Did one person hurt or upset the other (break something,
   etc.) by accident or on purpose?
How can you tell?
How else can you tell?
What might (the one hurt, etc.) do or say if the person
   hurt, broke something, etc., on purpose?
What might (the one hurt, etc.) do or say if the person
   hurt, broke something, etc., by accident?

Here are some scenarios you can suggest, if needed, in which
the intent of one child is ambiguous:

Two kids are roughhousing and one receives a black eye
Kids are playing basketball, and one boy knocks another
   down
A girl holding a valuable porcelain doll drops it and it breaks

Not only are physical acts—such as bumping or breaking—
sometimes misinterpreted, but non-physical social acts are misinterpreted as well. When shown a picture of a girl looking away
from a classmate standing next to her, Sarah assumed the girl was
being ignored. Donna noticed a smile on the girl's face and said,
"Maybe she's watching her friends doing (jump rope) tricks."
   If your child has not already done so, you can suggest that
she draw facial expressions on her characters, as well as any
other details that would reveal whether someone did something
on purpose or by accident. If necessary, ask her to retell the story
that includes these new cues.

Momentary Exchanges in Real Life

Finally, use opportunities that crop up during the day to discuss
motivation. Nicholas, for example, mentioned during dinner
that he was hit in the knee with a ball in gym class.

"What did you do or say next?" his mom asked.

"Nothing," Nicholas said, "because the kid said he was sorry."

"How did you know he was really sorry?" she asked.

"He looked sorry, and he came over and asked me if I was okay. If he wasn't sorry, he probably would have laughed, or just walked away without trying to help."

From this exchange, it's clear that Nicholas knows which cues are important, and how to interpret them correctly.

Sarah, however, has difficulty in this area. Her teacher called home after Sarah had lashed out mercilessly at Denise, one of her classmates. When her mother asked Sarah what had motivated her to lash out Sarah replied, "Denise frowned at me."

Typical of aggressive youngsters, Sarah had noticed the cue—Denise's facial expression—but considered only one interpretation: that the frown was directed at her. Thus, she responded with hostility instead of empathy, as aggressive children often do.

To make Sarah aware that facial expressions can be interpreted in more than one way, Sarah's mom asked, "Why else might Denise have frowned at you? Think real hard."

Sarah paused, and said softly, "Maybe someone bothered her?"

"Maybe," answered Sarah's mom. "That's one possible reason. Can you think of another?"

"Maybe she fell and hurt herself," Sarah said, starting to smile.

"How do you feel when you think of more than one reason someone does something?" her mother asked.

"Proud," answered Sarah. Sarah liked these questions very much.

Donna's family also had occasion to talk about how we interpret the actions of others when Donna came home from school one day in tears. Theresa, her new friend, didn't want to play with her. Donna thought Theresa didn't like her anymore, and nothing her mom could say would convince her otherwise. When Donna's mother tried the Explaining Approach, telling Donna that Theresa might not have been able to play with her on that day because she had to go to the doctor, or that perhaps she was tired, or had to study for a test, her explanations fell on deaf ears.

That's when Donna's mother changed tactics. She asked, "Can you think of any different reasons why Theresa didn't play with you today?"

Donna thought for a while, and then said, "Maybe her mother told her to come right home."

"Good thinking," said her mom, not wanting to push her any further right now. "You're starting to realize that there is more than one reason people do what they do."

Donna's making more progress now. And her mom was beginning to appreciate that asking, instead of explaining things to Donna, helped her daughter think more about why someone might do what they do.

Habitual Behavior Over Time: "Why Is He Like That?"

Trying to interpret another person's behavior over time involves a deeper level of insight than trying to determine a person's momentary intent. In the moment, we can ask questions, or watch for visual cues. But to understand why a person acts in a consistent way over a period of time, we need to understand another's underlying motives. The ability to look below the surface of human behavior and appreciate how it is often shaped by underlying and not obvious motives is a skill that helps children cope with others who behave in ways differently from them.

Suppose, for example, that ten-year-old James continually acts in dangerous ways. His friend Robert, who can evaluate behavior in terms of motivational insights, may think to himself, "James acts that way because he thinks it's fun" (a more superficial reason), or, attributing less obvious motives, "He's doing it so someone will take care of him if he's hurt," or "Maybe he's facing his fears." The last two reflect an awareness that there are explanations for James's behavior which aren't immediately apparent.

The goal of understanding underlying motives isn't to validate any of these explanations, but rather to acknowledge that there are often many hidden reasons why people act as they do.

Activities for Understanding Habitual Behavior

At any time the family is together, either parent can say, "Today let's talk about things people do and what makes them do these things. I'll start, and then you can join in. Let's say that Mark is always bragging about how smart he is. I'm going to ask some questions and anyone can answer." (Your spouse can join in but let your child or children answer most of the questions.)

> Why might someone brag about how smart he is?
> How might Mark feel when he brags like that?
> Is there any other possible way he might feel?
> How might other kids feel when he brags like that?
> What might other kids think when he brags like that?

Both Nicholas and Donna had some ideas that reflected deeper insight than did Sarah. Nicholas attributed Mark's bragging to a deep insecurity, saying, "Mark doesn't really feel smart, and bragging makes him feel smart." But Nicholas also recognized that Mark might feel frustrated because he knows he has trouble in school. Nicholas and Donna also reflected that other kids wouldn't like to be around Mark because all he does is talk about how great he is. As Donna noted, "That's why he doesn't have any friends."

Sarah could not see very far below the surface. She simply acknowledged, "Mark brags 'cause it makes him feel good."

Here's another scenario you can suggest: Suppose Eric, a fifth-grader, picks on the girls shooting baskets in the playground. He teases them every time they miss a shot by laughing and saying things like, "I can't believe you missed such an easy shot," or, "You're so clumsy."

When asked the same questions as in the previous scenario, Nicholas had many interpretations. Eric might act that way, Nicholas suggested, "Because he likes to be a big shot, he doesn't really like himself, people are mean to him, or he has a problem at home."

Donna also exhibited some insight when she suggested, "He's just mad at the world," or, "His mom beats him and he takes it out on his friends." But Sarah, like other aggressive children, took sides with the bully, explaining, "They can't shoot baskets and he can," and "Now they all know he's somebody."

What helped Sarah begin to recognize that there is more than one reason people do what they do was to create more scenarios herself. She enjoyed, for example, drawing a picture of a girl laughing and pointing her finger at another girl. The task engaged her much more than simply talking about such a scenario. When asked to explain the picture, Sarah said that one girl was teasing the other because she (the victim) was ugly. But then she explained that she (the perpetrator) is ugly too, and has no friends. This recognition—that the perpetrator may have teased the other girl because she felt bad about herself—was a breakthrough for Sarah, who was beginning to recognize possible reasons people do what they do beyond the most obvious.

Habitual Behavior in Real Life

When we deal with actual people, it's often difficult—if not impossible—to determine their underlying motives. Why does one child bully another? Why does a child take things without asking? These persistent, annoying, and sometimes harmful behaviors are hard to interpret. Yet it's still important that children try; they need to recognize that people act in a certain way for different reasons.

When Donna came home upset because a girl she doesn't like keeps pestering her to play, her mom asked her, "Why do you think she does that?"

"Because she likes to bother me," Donna said at first. But then, remembering that she had talked about these kinds of situations with her mother, she said, "Maybe she doesn't have any friends."

Her mom followed that with "Why Else?"

"Maybe she likes me."

"How do you feel when she pesters you?"

"Mad. She bothers me."

"What do you say to her now?"

"Nothing, I just walk away."

"How do you think she feels?"

"Sad."

Donna's mom then asked, "If you thought she was out to pester you, how would you treat her? Would that be different than if you thought she didn't have any friends, or that she really liked you and didn't know how to ask you to play with her?"

Donna replied, "I guess I'd be nicer if I thought she didn't have friends or if she didn't know how to ask me to play, but I still wouldn't be her friend."

Donna's mom didn't push any further for now. At least Donna was beginning to recognize that it was possible that the girl was not just out to pester her.

Sarah also showed a new measure of insight into why people behave as they do over time. One evening, she told her parents about a boy at school who "always has to win."

"Tell us more about him," her dad asked.

"When we win, he says we cheat. When he wins, it's 'cause he's good. He says, 'I'm the winner!' And I say, 'Yeah, you're the winner of the bragging contest.'"

Hardly able to suppress a smile, her mom asked, "Why do you think he does that?"

Sarah said, "'Cause he knows he can't win playing fair."

That was a good beginning. Sarah's parents were thrilled, and let the dialogue stop there.

Even children who do have insight into why others act as they do can have difficulty changing the way they feel about them. I asked Nicholas to tell me about Raymond, a classmate who is often very nasty to him. He said that if he knew that Raymond was "just acting like his father," he might feel more compassion for him, but added, "he's still not nice." Nicholas continued, "He thinks I'm very nosy when I just ask a simple question." When I asked Nicholas what he meant by that, he said, "I asked him what place he was doing [for a geography project] and Raymond acted like a real brat." The way Nicholas explained it to me, it seemed that Raymond had answered snidely, "Why do you have to know?" Nicholas "felt bad" because "I was just trying to be nice."

At this point, even Nicholas was unable to change the way he relates to children like Raymond. But children can learn to think about why people might do what they do. This and the other skills I have discussed so far—listening, and expressing and recognizing one's own and others' feelings—will give children the foundation to solve problems that come up with peers, their teachers, and their parents.

Summarizing Tips

Momentary Exchange:

- If your child is upset about what someone did or said, ask if she can remember everything the other person did or said, and whether there is any other possible reason for the action or the remark.

   Ask your child to tell you what she noticed about the other person's facial expression, tone of voice, or any body movements that might help give clues about the intent of that person.

   Ask your child what he did or said after the other child did what he did or said. Then ask your child whether he would have said or done the same thing if the intent was to hurt his feelings, or for a genuine reason; for example, not being able to keep a promise to play, go somewhere, etc.

   If the act was ambiguous in intent, ask your child if she would say or do anything different if she knew the other child intentionally meant to harm or whether what happened was an accident.

Habitual Behavior

- If your child complains about the habitual behavior of another, such as a child at school who perpetually bullies or teases, ask him to think about different possible reasons that child may act that way.

   Ask your child how the other child might feel when he does that.

Ask your child how he feels when the other child does that.

NOTE: *Helping children think more about what to do and say in response to bullies and teasers will give them problem-solving skills that are described in Chapters 6 and 7.*

• As parents, think about various possible reasons your children do what they do. If you have a child who bullies or teases others, for example, think about why she might be doing that. It is possible that your child may feel overpowered and has a need to regain control over her life. For now, just think about what you can do or say differently if your child is seeking attention, or whatever the reason might be. As we mentioned in Chapter 4, pay attention to nonverbal cues of your child, perhaps particularly your son, who may be hiding his inner feelings. Just as you are teaching your child that things may not always be what they seem to be, it is important for you to recognize that your child's feelings may not always be what *they* seem to be. (How to talk to your child to find out what's on his/her mind will be discussed in Chapter 6.)

◀ 6 ▶

What Else Could I Do to Solve This Problem? Learning Alternative Solutions

*Children who can solve their own problems feel
empowered, not overpowered.*

Sarah is starting to feel more comfortable letting people know
what's on her mind. She's also less resistant to others when
they let her know how they're feeling and what they're thinking.
Instead of shutting them out she seems more open to their feedback; she seems to care more about what other people have to
say. Rather than jump to quick and faulty conclusions, she is
more likely to think about why people do what they do.

This is an important first step on her journey toward social
competence. But it is not enough. Although Sarah is better able
to control her anger when aroused, and is able to refrain from
lashing out or calling someone a name when provoked, she still
cannot think of what else to do in these conflictual situations.

Donna is well aware of how others feel, but she is still afraid
to join others in play, and is still taken advantage of because she
can't yet stand up for her rights with peers. She gives up too
soon, and, like Sarah, is unable to think of what else to do.

What most distinguishes Nicholas from Sarah and Donna is
his ability to relieve his own and others' tensions when a conflict
arises. He knows how to use his listening skills and his sensitivity

to others to solve the problem. But as I mentioned in Chapter 1, there are always times when even the best problem solvers like Nicholas don't use the skills they have.

In this and the next three chapters, I will show you how to help your children become active participants in the problem-solving process and how to reduce tension when conflicts arise. Whether your child has a problem with a sibling, a friend, a teacher, or with you, everyone can end up feeling good.

Learning to Think of Alternative Solutions

Children who are socially and emotionally competent are able to think of different ways to solve problems rather than reacting impulsively or giving up if the first attempt should fail. For example, such a child might think that to make new friends, she could:

- Offer to share something of hers
- Have a party
- Meet new girls at school

To encourage your child to come up with different solutions to a problem, think of it as a brainstorming session. That's when people agree to suspend judgment and offer a variety of possible solutions, no matter how far-fetched. The goal is to think of as many options as possible in response to a specific task or problem: "I could do this, or that, or I could even do that . . ."

Some of you know from my first book, *Raising a Thinking Child*, that the ability to generate different solutions is critical throughout life. Children as young as three or four are capable of this skill. But skill training doesn't stop there. It's important that children continue to develop and sharpen this skill as they grow so they can draw on it in their increasingly complex day-to-day lives. And if thinking of alternative solutions is new to your child, then ages eight to twelve isn't too late to start. First, practice using fictitious situations, then real ones.

Using Alternative Solutions in Fictitious Situations

It's often best to start helping your child learn this skill by encouraging her to think about other people's problems, or problems involving fictitious characters. This way, she won't feel as anxious as she might if she were to consider real problems in her actual life. Even if your child can think of an example that really happened to her and wants to use it, she may eventually clam up as she recalls the tension of the experience. That's why I recommend beginning with fictitious characters.

First, review earlier ICPS exercises. You can say, "When we played the How Can This Be? game (in Chapter 4), or the Why Else? game (in Chapter 5), what we were *really* doing was asking if there was more than one way to figure out what people are thinking and feeling. There's also *more than one* way to solve a problem that comes up between people. First, I'm going to tell you a problem between two made-up kids. Alex (or Margaret) and Bob (or Janine) are both (*age of your child*). Alex wants Bob to be his friend. What can Alex do or say so that Bob will be his friend?"

After your child names one solution, say: "That's one way. The idea of this game is to think of lots of *different* ways to solve this problem. There are no right or wrong answers. Tell me anything else you can think of."

Sarah was surprised when her mom didn't disparage her for saying, "Tell her she'll beat her up if she won't be her friend." Instead of commenting on her thoughts about her daughter's solution, Sarah's mother simply said, "That's *one* way. Can you

think of lots of ways?" This freed Sarah to think of other possibilities.

"Ask her, and if she says no, ask her why," Sarah said.

Her mom replied, "That's two ways. What's a third?"

Sarah paused to really think about this, and said, "Say funny
things to get her attention."

Sarah's mother was pleased with Sarah—not because of the
content of what she said, but because she was able to come up
with more than one way to solve a problem. She was also pleased
with her own response. In the past, she would have been more
judgmental. Now she realized that when she reacted to one of
Sarah's solutions by saying, "No, don't do that," or "Very good,"
or "I like that one," Sarah would be tempted to follow through
on her mother's feedback. Then, if the solutions her mother had
praised didn't work, Sarah would find herself at a dead end
because she hadn't generated alternative solutions during the
brainstorming phase.

And Donna thought of, "She could talk to her about her
problems." When asked for more, Donna added, "Carry her
books when she's tired," and "Say, 'I've never had a friend
before.'"

Children like Sarah and Donna don't spontaneously come up
with three or four solutions when asked about fictitious characters. But if they are urged to think of more responses, they can
generate them. Nicholas, in contrast, can usually think of many
solutions on his own. Here are some of his suggestions: "Keep
him from stealing something," "Protect him if someone's bothering him," and "Ask him for advice when he has a problem."
Another ICPS child, a twelve-year-old girl, offered, "Arrange for
someone to threaten to beat her up, and then make a trap and
save her from it." This is a good example of how competent children can think of an idea that parents might not favor. In this situation, her mother, without interrupting the flow of ideas, asked
her daughter to think of even more ideas. The girl then added,

"Vote her into the kid's club," "Ease into it bit by bit," and "Get her to trust her."

But even competent children of this age tend to include solutions with the same theme. In response to the example above, Nicholas offered, "Tell him he plays a great game of soccer," and, "Tell him he's the funniest boy in class." Though seemingly different, these answers are both variations on the theme of flattering. To help your child get over this mental roadblock, you can say, "Telling him he plays a great game of soccer and telling him he's the funniest boy in class are both forms of flattering him. Can you think of something different from *flattering* him?"

Let your child draw characters or stick figures and make up a problem of her own. One girl, age eleven, drew the ones below, and said, "Georgette is upset because her friend is mad at her."

Her mom asked, "What can Georgette do or say so her friend won't be mad?"

"She could buy her her favorite ice cream."

"What else?"

"She could help her with her homework. Or she could ask her to please not be mad. Or she could get her other friends to tell her she's sorry."

She, like Nicholas, could think of many answers when asked.

Understanding that Donna was still fearful of others—especially if she thought someone was angry with her—her mom created a different problem situation, and then added a new question to this exercise. She told Donna that Ruth's brother has been pestering her a lot lately when she wants to do her homework. She asked Donna to think about what Ruth could do or say so her brother would stop bothering her during homework time. Donna's mom asked her to first think of only those solutions that might *not* make her brother feel angry and then, solutions that *might* make her brother feel angry.

Donna said, "She could tell him she needs to study 'cause she needs a good education."

"That's one idea," said her mom. "What else could she do or say?"

"She could say that she'll play with him after she's done her homework," Donna replied. When asked, she couldn't think up any other solutions for now. Then her mother asked her what Ruth could say that might make her brother feel angry, and Donna said, "Tell him she'll play now, but she only pretends to follow him outside, and then she shuts the door in his face."

"Yes, that might make her brother angry," Donna's mom said. "What's another way to make him angry?"

Donna thought and said, "Tell him to go away!"

Sarah's mom used this exercise to help her reflect on how different kinds of solutions can affect the feelings of others. Sarah was now ready to make these distinctions, but only in fictitious situations. When asked, Sarah said that Ruth's brother would not be angry if "Ruth let him play with her video games while she does her homework," and he would be angry if Ruth's friends "ganged up on him." Then she giggled, and said, "Ruth could also hide under the bed so he can't find her, but I don't know if that would make him angry or not." Her mom laughed too, adding, "It would probably only be funny if he found her there!" Her mother hoped soon Sarah would be able to make these distinctions when her own younger brother "bugged her."

When Nicholas was asked to name two ways that Robert could explain to his sister that he needed to do his homework, he was typically creative. "She wouldn't be angry if he told her a little story about a friend who always bugs someone," he said first. He also said that Robert could get his sister interested in Legos, and show her how to make a Lego airplane. "Then," he explained, "she could work on the plane, and Robert could do his homework." Asked what would make Robert's sister angry, Nicholas said, "If he gives her all the wrong answers, she'll never bug him again," and "Take her someplace and leave her there." Nicholas chuckled as he said this, saying, "She'll know she was duped."

Children also enjoy coming up with different solutions to problems that arise on the situation comedies they watch on TV, or in the books they read. You can make up problems while riding in the car, at the dinner table—anywhere that is conducive to conversation. Donna, who still preferred writing to talking, created her own special diary for ICPS and entered this exercise. She made up problems, sketched characters, and wrote down several solutions. One day she felt so proud of her accomplishments that she came running to both her mom and dad and showed them her drawings. For the first time, she enjoyed reading her ideas out loud, perhaps because she had already composed her answers, and didn't have to think on her feet. Whatever the reason, Donna was talking and laughing and feeling very proud.

With this exercise under their belts, Donna, Sarah, and Nicholas were ready to practice the skill of thinking of more than one way to solve problems that arose in their real lives.

In Real Life

As I mentioned in Chapter 1, problems and conflicts naturally and inevitably occur daily in children's lives. The goal is not to get rid of all conflict, but to learn how to competently and confidently cope. There are three major arenas in which children usually encounter conflict: with other kids, with their parents, and with teachers. I will discuss this last conflict in the next chapter.

Problems between Children

When I asked children eight through twelve years old to tell me which problems most concern them in terms of other children, the problem of bullies topped the list.

One very popular and socially skilled ten-year-old couldn't get Dominique, the class bully, off her mind. Even when we talked about other things, such as her new love for ice-skating, Dominique would always creep back into the conversation. As I talked with this girl, I began to realize that her preoccupation with Dominique had two components. First, she was afraid of the girl. But she also felt helpless because she didn't know how to get Dominique out of her hair.

Bullies are bothersome to boys as well. Even good problem solvers like Nicholas have a hard time handling an overly aggressive child. Here's how Nicholas's mother talked to him to help him focus on finding different solutions to this very real problem:

> *Mom*: I know that Andrew bothers you when he acts like a bully. What can you think of to do or say so he won't bully you?
> *Nicholas*: I could just stay away from him.
> *Mom*: Okay, that's *one* thing you can do. What else can you do?

(*Nicholas thought for a moment.*)
Nicholas: I could tell him I feel mad when he bothers me.

The next day, Nicholas actually told Andrew how angry he was when Andrew bothered him—but because he was a little afraid of Andrew, he had the conversation on the playground, when other kids were nearby. Andrew, like most aggressive children, was not particularly concerned about Nicholas's feelings, and continued to bother him. Nevertheless, Nicholas was still glad that he'd told Andrew how he felt. Though Nicholas wished he could change Andrew so he wouldn't be a bully anymore, this wasn't a realistic goal. All that Nicholas could do was find a way to cope with the problem, whether by avoiding Andrew, or by explaining how he felt and feeling relieved.

Sarah was becoming more empathic. She was beginning to understand how people felt when she tormented or teased them. And because she had been learning to think about what to do or say when someone else acted in those ways toward her, she was able to appreciate, for the first time, how others view her when she behaves in those ways. She recognized that her classmates didn't want to play with her, confide in her, or work with her on group projects, as much as she wished they would. But now she was starting to understand the role she herself played in being excluded. As a mark of her progress, Sarah began noticing when other girls acted as she had, and noted the consequences. For example, upon noticing that a girl in her class was bullying others, she thought of saying, "You won't have any friends if you bother people like that."

Although Sarah was now paying attention to her own feelings and was better able to attend to those of others, she still had trouble controlling her emotions in the heat of a conflict. One day, both she and her father had the opportunity to learn to approach conflict in a different, more thoughtful way.

Sarah's dad got a note from her teacher that she was bullying a classmate who didn't want to share her magic marker. His first reaction was to lash out—to tell Sarah that she'd done the wrong thing, that she wouldn't have any friends if she persisted in bullying—and to punish her. But because he was learning ICPS, he stopped himself and began a problem-solving dialogue.

Dad: What happened? What was the problem?

Sarah: I wanted the marker and Joni wouldn't give it to me!

Dad: And then what happened?

Sarah: I called her stupid and gave her a look and she got scared.

Dad: Can you think of a way to get her to share the marker that is different from scaring her?

Sarah, sensing her father would not criticize her, felt less tense and thought hard about what else she could do. She said, "Break the marker and then she couldn't have it either." Sarah's father hadn't expected this response, but he remembered the exercise used for fictitious situations.

Dad: Would scaring her and breaking the marker make Joni feel angry or not angry?

Sarah: Angry, I guess.

Dad: Now can you think of solutions that would *not* make Joni feel angry?

Sarah: NO.

Feeling frustrated, her father took a deep breath and waited until he calmed down before speaking. Finally, he said, "I know if you think very hard, you can think of an idea."

Sarah, who was surprised her father wasn't yelling at her, said, "I could ask her."

Her dad smiled. "Good thinking," he said.

Note that Sarah's dad didn't praise *what* she thought, but *that* she thought. He didn't push any further for now.

The next day, Sarah came home very excited and said, "Dad, I told Joni I was sorry I scared her."

What a moment!

Donna also told her parents about a girl who picks on her in class, but when asked to come up with ideas for handling this situation, she said, "You can't stop someone from doing what they want to do." Perhaps Donna could not yet think of what she could do or say when confronted by a bully. Perhaps she just preferred to avoid confrontation at all costs.

Because Donna was still shy and fearful of others, helping her take control at this juncture was especially important. Children who are bullied often feel helpless, and this feeling can linger for a lifetime. Sometimes, these very children who could not at first defend themselves become bullies themselves. That's why Donna's mother refused to take Donna's initial response, "I don't know"—at face value. Instead, she brainstormed with her daughter to come up with alternative solutions, using the Problem-Solving Approach.

> *Mom*: I know if you try hard, you can think of something. It doesn't matter what it is. Make up anything for now.
>
> *Donna*: I could tell the teacher.
>
> *Mom*: That's one way. Can you think of another way?
>
> *Donna*: Tell you.

This response gave Donna's mother pause. She realized that in the past, she'd tried to protect her timid daughter from being victimized by saying, "Don't worry, I'll talk to your teacher about this." By doing so, Donna didn't have to figure out what to say or how to act—her mother solved her problems for her. Now, thanks to ICPS, Donna's mother recognized that for

Donna, telling the teacher and telling her mother were variations on the same theme, and that Donna needed to think of a new strategy. So she said to Donna, "Telling the teacher and telling me are both examples of the same idea—you tell someone. Can you think of something different from telling someone?"

"Yeah, I could tell her to stop picking on me," Donna said. She was clearly surprised that she'd been able to come up with such a thought. Although she wasn't yet ready to act on it, she was starting to realize that things don't have to just happen to her; she could make things happen too.

Donna then went to her room, opened her ICPS diary, and started writing down more ideas. For the first time, she was beginning to feel more confident—something she could never feel when her parents tried to soothe her by saying, "Ignore it," "You don't want friends like that," or "I'll talk to your teacher about it."

But neither children nor parents change completely overnight. A couple of weeks later, Donna came home crying:

Donna: Mom, I thought I could trust Tracey and now I know I can't.
Mom: What happened?
Donna: She told Tammy I don't like it when she teases me.
Mom: Well, tell Tracey you don't like what she did.
Donna: I can't. She'll start teasing me too.
Mom: You're getting to be a big girl now. You have to learn to defend yourself.

Without realizing it, her mom had reverted back to doing the thinking for Donna when she said, "Well, tell Tracey you don't like what she did."

Fortunately, she caught herself. Remembering the Problem-Solving Approach, Donna's mom realized that her job was to help Donna think of alternative solutions to a problem.

Mom: Tracey told someone something you wanted kept
secret. How does that make you feel?

Donna: Angry, and disappointed. A little scared too.

Mom: What can you do or say so Tracey will know how
you feel about this?

Donna: I can tell her I feel angry and disappointed. But I
won't tell her I'm scared.

Mom: Good thinking. Go ahead and try that.

The next day, Donna proudly reported that she told Tracey
she felt angry and disappointed that Tracey had betrayed her
secret, and that Tracey said she was sorry. Free to think of her own
solution, with guidance from Mom, Donna felt capable of taking
action on her own, and the pride she felt was its own reward.

Another problem many eight- to twelve-year-olds encounter
involves competition, either between themselves and kids at
school, or at home with siblings. Everyone feels exasperated at
times, including socially competent children like Nicholas.
Encouraging children to think of different ways to diffuse competition is just as important for Nicholas as it is for Sarah and
Donna.

Nicholas still flies off the handle, especially when he senses
that his sister is competing with him, even over little things like
helping to bake cookies. As he says, "Every time I start to pour
the stuff, Tara wants to pour it too. She's always in my hair. I get
out my video game, and she wants to play with it."

During one cookie-making session, when Nicholas yelled,
"Tara, get out of my hair, you're bugging me again!" his mom
put out the fire by asking one simple question: "Nicholas, can
you think of a different way to tell your sister how you feel?"

After he calmed down, Nicholas said, "Okay, Tara, you can
pour the stuff first this time." Though he still felt frustrated, he
told his mom that he knew his sister would soon be bored with
her task, and then he could have his turn.

Nicholas was also put out when Tara wanted to go with him to his friend's house. He told her, "I want to talk about things and I don't want you there." That didn't faze Tara; she still insisted on going. Nicholas then said, "You're a girl. Girls don't play with boys." That made Tara more defiant still.

One day a friend invited Tara to play at her house, and Nicholas said, "I'll come with you." Tara said, "No, I don't want you to come there." Suddenly, it dawned on Nicholas that he had stumbled on a solution to his problem with his sister. He said to her, "Now you know how I feel when I want my privacy with my friends." Having seen the situation from her brother's point of view, Tara stopped bothering him about this.

Sarah got caught up in competition at school. Several times over the past couple of months, she found herself arguing with her friends over who has better clothes. As a result, she began to lobby her mother to buy her more expensive pants, tops, and shoes. Her mother felt torn. On the one hand, she was happy that Sarah was starting to care about making friends. On the other hand, she wished that Sarah wouldn't put so much stock in using clothes to impress her peers. At the same time, she knew that the clothes Sarah wanted were beyond the scope of the family budget.

But because Sarah's mother was encouraged that her daughter had stopped lashing out, she began to talk to her about how to solve the problem facing her.

Mom: What could you do or say so the kids won't brag about their clothes?

Sarah: I could just tell them their clothes are ugly. No, I've got a better idea. I could just tell them they don't know what they're talking about. That would make me feel better inside.

Mom (*drawing from the question used in fictitious situations*): Would those solutions make them feel angry or not angry?

Sarah: Angry, I guess, but I can't think of anything else.

Mom: You're getting good at this. I know you can think of something.

Sarah: I could tell them I like my clothes and to stop showin' off.

Mom: Now you're thinking of more ideas. What else can you think of?

Sarah: I could get the other kids to tell them to stop. I know. I could get the teacher to give them a harder time so I don't have to deal with that.

Then Sarah smiled a little and said, "But I guess that would make them angry, wouldn't it."

Her mom felt very proud that Sarah knew, without being prompted, what would make the other girls angry.

Donna wasn't trying to outdo anyone or compete about clothes, yet she felt particularly sad when a classmate told her she wasn't very good at drawing. Instead of focusing on what she could *not* do, her mom said, "Think of *one* thing you are very good at." Although Donna didn't answer at that moment, she took out her diary that night and started to think of things she could say or do to feel better.

A week later, just before Christmas, Donna had an idea. She asked her mom to help her bake a gingerbread man. She shaped a mouth with sugar and put it on the figure's forehead. Candy ball eyes went under his mouth, and his licorice nose went under his right eye. Donna laughed so hard she could hardly stop. She couldn't wait to go to school the next day to show off her creation. All the kids laughed, and Donna came home beaming. Finally, she'd been noticed.

Donna's mother learned an important lesson along with her daughter. Had her mother suggested the gingerbread idea, Donna would likely have cast it aside. But this had been Donna's idea. She felt safe, and ready to give it a try.

Problems between Parent and Child

Though the Power, Suggesting, and Explaining Approaches differ in many ways, they have one feature in common: they don't involve conversation, but rely instead on monologues. All too often, parents find themselves talking to themselves, more engaged with the agenda in their own heads than with the child to whom they are purportedly speaking.

Eleven-year-old Randy and his mother found themselves entangled in a recurring problem about his going to R-rated and frightening movies with his friends. Here's how their dialogue went:

Randy: I'm going to the movies on Saturday with my friends.
Mom: What are you going to see?
Randy: Psycho.
Mom: I don't want you to see that. You'll have nightmares.
Randy: Mom, everybody's going. If I don't go with my friends, I'll never be popular.
Mom: RANDALL! (*She's really angry.*)
Randy: Mom, please, I already called everybody. I promised them I'd go.
Mom: If you have to worry about going to a certain movie to be popular, maybe you're hanging out with the wrong friends. Friendship is based on who you are; it's about trust, and being genuine with each other. If it's just based on superficial things, it's not a true friendship. Your friends like you for who you are, no matter what.

Randy's mother told me that she had this discussion with her son several times, and now he understands why he doesn't have to follow the crowd.

Now let's see how Randy interpreted this "discussion." Here's how he thought the interchange took place:

Randy: Mom, I'm going to the movies on Saturday night.
Mom: What are you going to see?
Randy: *Psycho*.
Mom: No, I don't want you seeing that.
Randy: Mom, everybody's going. If I can't go with my friends, I'm never going to be popular.
Mom: RANDALL!
Randy: I already read the book. It's no big deal.
Mom: RANDALL. I don't want you to see *Psycho*!
Randy (*to me*): All she does is get mad. Sometimes she lets me go and sometimes she doesn't.

I asked him what happens next when his mom really means "no," and he said, "I raise my voice and go to my room."

Notice that Randy did not mention one word of Mom's long explanation about friendship. There's a good chance he didn't hear a word of it. He also didn't mention her reason for not wanting him to see the movie. All he heard was her anger, which he exaggerated.

Although Randy's mom's use of the Power Approach was minimal, Randy's perception of his mother's anger superceded her Explanations because he saw that as what blocked him from satisfying his immediate need.

Randy's mother was surprised and disappointed that her son did not remember one word of her explanations. This created an impetus for her to use the Problem-Solving Approach with Randy, and she soon came to see how involving her son in the resolution of the problem might prevent him from tuning out.

Mom: Randy, is following the crowd the only way for you to be popular?

Randy: Mom, they'll think I'm a geek if I don't go.

Mom: Can you think of a different way to show them you're not a geek?

Randy: NO! I have to go to the movie.

Mom (*not giving up*): I know you can think of a way. What do *you* like to do?

Randy: You know I like hockey.

(*Mom looks at her son with a knowing smile.*)

Randy (*excitedly*): Mom, I know. I can show them how to play hockey.

Randy's mom guided her son toward a solution with her question, "What do *you* like to do?" I was pleased that she was able to refrain from suggesting the solution herself, especially since this was the first time she'd tried an ICPS dialogue. And she was pleased that Randy was able to think about something other than his intense need to "follow the crowd."

Does the Explaining Approach work? Let's see what happened when Scott's mom tried that.

Scott, who was ten, never wanted to take a shower, and his mother was frantic. When I asked her how she handled her son's resistance, she told me that she would say to him, "If you don't take a shower, no one will want to be around you. You won't have any friends. You'll get sick . . ." Of course, the more she *explained*, the more Scott dug in his heels.

I urged her to ask Scott one simple question: "Why don't you want to take a shower?" If nothing else, this would allow Scott to get a word in edgewise. And sure enough, he answered: "It isn't fun."

"Well, I have to go to work and that isn't fun," his mother began—but then she stopped herself. She knew that this response was more about her anger than her son's reluctance, so she asked a different question: "What can you do to make it fun?"

Scott thought for a moment, and then said, "I can pretend I'm under a waterfall in Hawaii." Not only did he think his idea was funny, but he thought of it himself. That day, Scott willingly took a shower.

We all need to realize what Scott's mom did—if we want our children to listen to us, we must show them that we are listening to them.

It will come as no surprise that the major area of contention between parents and kids is bedroom messiness. Most kids feel as if their room is their business, and parents have no right demanding that it look a certain way. Parents argue that the house belongs to the family and that certain minimum standards must be maintained. Clearly, parents and children have different points of view about the same thing. And neither sees the viewpoint of the other. How do most families cope?

Donna's mother used to give her an icy stare coming into her bedroom, and Donna would respond by straightening up. This made Donna's mom think her strategy was effective. But was it? Was she really accomplishing her main goal? Was Donna keeping her room clean because *she* wanted to, or because her mother insisted on it? What will she do later on, when no one is around to demand a clean room? And how did Donna feel inside after she received one of her mother's stares?

Sarah's mother also used the Power Approach. She'd say, "It's important to me that your room is picked up. It makes me *crazy* to see such a mess!" This made Sarah angrier, and one day she shouted, "It's my room. I can do what I want in *my* room!"

In turn, her mom's fury grew, and she shouted, "I got you all this stuff. You wouldn't even have a room if it weren't for me!"

But Sarah tuned this out. She just didn't want to hear it.

Nicholas also liked his room sloppy. His mother tried the Explaining Approach, telling Nicholas that if he wanted to grow up to be a responsible adult, he had to develop good habits now.

None of these methods was particularly effective—but ICPS *can* help get parents and kids off their collision course.

The first step for parents is to realize that the goal is not to let children do whatever they want. If parents want a clean room, children do not choose whether to clean it. However, they can choose *how* to clean it. Sarah's mom, for example, helped her think about how to satisfy her needs while appreciating her mother's feelings as well. She told her daughter, "You can decide where to put your stuffed animals and in which drawer you want to put your socks. Just start with one thing at a time."

Even if only one corner of the room was picked up that day, Sarah's mom had given control of the task back to her daughter, and Sarah, for her part, assumed the responsibility her mother wanted her to assume—but in her way, and at her pace.

Sarah could hold on to the feeling that her room was her own private domain while acceding to her parents' wishes. Best of all, Sarah's mom came to understand her daughter's point of view while Sarah came to understand and appreciate her mother's. Instead of feeling bombarded by commands, demands, and threats, Sarah was freed to make her own decisions about how her room would be arranged. She felt proud.

The same principle applies to other household chores. Nicholas and his dad tussled each fall when it was time to rake the leaves. Nicholas's dad thought that Nicholas should take responsibility for this chore, and wouldn't help him. As a result, the leaves accumulated to such an extent that Nicholas felt overwhelmed and didn't know where to begin. Each day, he'd tell his dad he "forgot" to rake. Then, his dad would ground him—sometimes for as long as a week. You can well imagine what thoughts were festering inside Nicholas's mind as he watched his friends play outdoors while he had to stay inside.

Finally, his dad decided to try an ICPS dialogue:

Dad: What can you do so you'll remember to rake the leaves?

Nicholas: I can write myself a note.

Dad: That's good thinking. Let's see how many ideas you can think of.

Nicholas: I can put the rake outside the garage door and then I'll see it when I come home. I can say, "Rake the leaves" ten times when I go to bed and then I'll remember it in the morning.

Clearly, it was never that Nicholas *couldn't* think of ideas, but rather that he *wouldn't* think of them when he felt belittled. The ICPS dialogue gave him an opportunity to feel resourceful, not humiliated.

Many parents speak to me about similar issues of responsibility. A mother of an eight-year-old told me how she used to handle the situation when her child refused to help with the dishes before she found ICPS:

Mom: Charise, you didn't help with the dishes.

Charise: I've got too much homework.

Mom: You've got a job to do around here. I feel bad that you don't care enough about our household to do your share.

Charise: Okay.

Because her mom used the Explaining Approach, Charise knew what her mom was feeling. But what did Charise's mom actually accomplish? Did she know what Charise was thinking? Next time, Charise's mom tried a different tack.

Mom: What's on your mind? You didn't help with the dishes tonight.

Charise: I've got too much homework.
Mom: Oh, we have a problem. How can we solve it?
Charise: I can trade turns with Bobby.
Mom: That's one way. How can you find out if that's okay with him?
Charise: I can ask him.
Mom: And if he says no, what else can you do?
Charise: I can watch less TV.
Mom: Good thinking. You decide how you can do it.

With no demanding, yelling, or belittling, Charise was free to solve her own problem.

Failing to return home from school at the expected time is another problem that frequently occurs beginning at about age ten, although it does occur in children even younger. A mom in ICPS training gets panic-stricken when her twelve-year-old doesn't come home on time, something that has happened more than once. Before we met her, she talked to her son this way:

Mom: Where have you been? It's four-thirty!
Child: I forgot what time it was.
Mom: Don't you know we were worried sick!
Child: I'm sorry.
Mom: Don't ever do that again, or you're in real trouble!

This mom was understandably acting out of worry, relief, and exasperation. When it happened again, however, she tried using the Problem-Solving Approach, focusing on talking about people's feelings and solutions to problems.

Mom: How do you think we feel when we don't know where you are this late?
Child: Worried, maybe mad.

Mom: What can you do so we won't worry and we'll know where you are?

Child: I could call you. But I was afraid you'd say come home now.

Mom: I might have said that. Why do you think we want you to call when you want to stay after school late?

Child: So you won't worry.

This child was helped to see beyond his own point of view. His mom had feelings too.

When children think of their own solutions to everyday conflicts, they begin to feel empowered, not overpowered.

Summing Up

- Conflicts are normal. Through conflict, children learn to negotiate their interpersonal world. View them as an opportunity from which to learn, not annoyances to be dealt with quickly and forgotten.

- After your child offers his first solution, validate it, *no matter what the content*. It's important to keep the flow of ideas coming, unimpeded. You can do this by saying, "That's *one* way." Then ask your child to think of different ways.

- Remember, it's the process of thinking of more than one idea that will help solve problems. For now, what your child thinks is less important than *that* he thinks. If you want to praise her for a particular solution, say, "Good thinking," not "That's a good idea." A "good idea" may work one time but not the next time, and this will leave the child stymied as to what to do next.

- After your child is comfortable brainstorming different solutions, ask him to think about how each solution might make others feel.

Considering solutions in light of how others might feel is the first way a child can learn to evaluate for himself whether a solution is good or not. In the next chapter, we'll see how a child can also evaluate her own solutions in light of other things that might happen next—the potential consequences of an act—including how those consequences might make *her* feel as well.

◀ 7 ▶

What Might Happen Next?
Learning Consequential Thinking

*Instead of us telling kids what and what not to do, and
why—kids can learn to think about what and what not
to do, and why.*

Thinking of different solutions to a problem, as we explored
in the last chapter, is an important skill—one which both
Sarah and Donna are learning, and at which Nicholas is improving. All three children can now figure out for themselves what to
do if they want something a friend has, or when they feel
betrayed, or victimized. Even if their first attempt is not successful, they don't give up or fly off the handle. Now, they can think
of alternative strategies.

But this is only part of the process of resolving a problem.
Besides asking, "What else can I do?" it's equally important to
ask: "What might happen next if I do that?"

We have already begun to consider how our behavior influ-
ences the way other people feel—which in itself can be a consequence of what we do. But up to now, we have focused on
making people angry. Now we will help children learn to pay
attention to a fuller spectrum of feelings, and to consider other
potential consequences of their behavior as well.

Remember when Sarah tried to get her classmate to give her
a marker by intimidating the girl? If Sarah had said to herself, "If

I scare her, she'll get back at me," she might have tried to come up with a different option. If Donna had been able to realize that she'd be embraced rather than rejected by her peers on the playground, maybe she would have been more willing to ask if she could play. Nicholas also needs help with this skill, for although he's capable of thinking about the impact of his actions on others, he doesn't always consider it in the heat of the moment.

Learning to Think of Consequences to Actions

It Takes Time to Think

By age eight, children can begin to realize that the first idea that comes to them may not always be the best one. To introduce this concept, start with an activity that you can call, "What's First?" Present your child with a problem, such as, "Rudy's teasing Timothy again. Tell me, *very quickly*, what Timothy can say or do so Rudy will stop teasing him." If your child pauses, say, "Tell me very quickly. What's his solution?"

Sarah immediately said, "Tell him, 'Get out of my face!'"

Donna chose, "Tell the teacher."

Nicholas thought of, "Say, 'Stop that!'"

Whatever your child says, you reply, 'Okay. Now let's do this again, only this time stop and think of another idea. Take your time and think. When you have another idea, tell me what it is." When your child responds, ask: "Which idea do you think is better—the first or second?"

After your child answers, ask, "Why do you think that?" The idea behind this exercise is to help children recognize that the first quickly-thought-of solution may not always be the best one. However, if your child insists that the first idea is unmistakably the best, you can still ask, "Can you think of a time when you did something to solve a problem and later thought of a better way?" If your child remembers such an incident, then say, "Sometimes it takes time to think and the first thing that comes into your head may not be the best idea."

Consequences for Fictitious Characters

Try this game when you're sitting together at the dinner table, or in the car, or anywhere conversation is possible. Begin by saying, "Remember when we talked about the time when Ruth's brother was being a pest while she was trying to do her homework? Now we're going to change the game. We're going to think of different things that might happen if Ruth actually did those things you said she could do."

Donna's mom said, "You said that Ruth could tell her brother she needs to study because she needs to get a good education. Now, do you think this was a good idea or not a good idea?"

"Good idea," said Donna, smiling.

"Why is that a good idea?" asked Mom.

Donna replied, " 'Cause then he'd understand and let her do her homework."

Next, her mom reminded Donna of a solution Donna had given that might make Ruth's brother angry: "Tell him she'll play now and when he goes outside, she'll shut the door." Then, she asked Donna whether that was a good idea or not, and Donna said, "Good idea?"

"Why do you think that?" asked Mom.

"Because then Ruth could get her homework done." This response gave Donna's mom information she could not have learned had she commented on *her* opinion of that solution. Even though Donna was aware of other people's feelings, as we saw earlier, she was not always able to draw upon that knowledge in problem situations, even fictitious ones. Donna was focusing on *her* needs, not the impact of her solution on another person. Her mom hadn't realized this.

With the new insight into how Donna was thinking about it, her mom asked, "I know you're aware that this idea might make her brother angry. We talked about that before. Now I want you to think of something new. Think about other things that might happen next after Ruth shut the door on him, things other than how he might feel."

"Her dad might spank her," replied Donna.

"Okay, that might happen. What else might happen?" When Donna told her she didn't know, her mom added, "What might Ruth's brother do or say if Ruth says she'll play and then shuts the door?"

"Maybe he'll say that he'll never play with her again."

"Do you think Ruth would like that?"

"No," said Donna.

"Okay, which idea do you think is better, to tell him she needs to study because she needs a good education, or to tell him she'll play and then shut the door?"

Donna thought for a moment, and said, "Tell him she needs a good education." Donna has always been aware of how other people feel in problem situations. She was now beginning to understand what to do about those feelings, and what might happen if she follows through.

When Sarah had been asked about this situation, she had said that Ruth "could let her brother play with her video games while she does her homework," a solution that would not make her brother angry, and "get her friends to gang up on him," a solution that Sarah acknowledged would. When Sarah's mother asked her which one she thought was better, Sarah recognized that the first was better than the second, but thought that "her friends ganging up on him" was very funny.

Her mom then asked, "What else might happen if her friends did that?" This question caused Sarah to think, for the first time, about not only another's feelings, but other consequences as well. She replied, "He might think no one likes him anymore."

In both cases, Donna and Sarah were asked to evaluate their own ideas, rather than being told whether their ideas were good or bad. In the process, they stretched their thinking to uncharted territory. They were beginning to see how their own needs meshed with the needs of others, so everyone involved comes out on top.

To prepare their children to apply this new skill to real life, Donna's and Sarah's moms gave them practice with one more situation involving fictitious characters: "James was very mad at his friend Karen, and told her off. What might happen next?"

This situation was difficult for Donna. She said, "Karen will yell back at him and then hide." Typically, Donna was still trying to avoid confrontation.

Sarah had an easier time thinking about this since she herself had suffered the consequences of this behavior quite often. In fact, she'd been in this exact situation, yet she was able to talk about it freely because the characters were presented as fictitious. She didn't feel as if she was talking directly about herself.

"They'll fight," Sarah said. When asked what else might happen, Sarah replied, "James will feel sorry he scared her." Sarah's mother was astonished by this. "He'll feel sorry . . ." and ". . . he scared her" were empathic responses. It indicated that Sarah was thinking about both her own and the other's feelings at the same time. After a few more seconds she added, completely on her own, "I guess telling her off wasn't a good idea."

"And what is a good idea?"

"They could just talk it out," Sarah said. Sarah's mom stopped here, trying to remain calm in the face of Sarah's breakthrough. She was very proud of her daughter.

Here are some interesting consequences that Andrea, from the last chapter, gave to this situation: "Karen tells James, 'I thought we were friends, but friends don't tell each other off,'" and "Karen might tell him she's not his friend anymore." But she was also able to think of two very empathic consequences: "Karen might feel embarrassed, ashamed, or upset," and "James might feel bad that he told Karen off."

When Nicholas's mother suggested practicing this skill, Nicholas created a problem of his own. He wrote a story about a boy who always butted into other people's play at recess, a story I modified for the "I Can Problem Solve" program now being used in intermediate elementary school grades. He called his story, "Bucky Butt-er-in-er." Here it is.

> (*Craig and Michael are playing ball.*)
> *Craig*: Bucky, you're butting in our game!
> *Mike*: You always butt in, and we don't like that. Go away!
> *Bucky*: Ha, ha. You can't even catch a ball.
> *Craig*: If you keep buttin' in, you can never play with us.
> *Bucky*: If you let me play with you, you can use my bat.
> *Craig*: If it's okay with Mike.
> *Bucky* (*to Mike*): I'll let you play with my bat too.
> *Mike*: Okay. But don't ever butt in again.

Nicholas's parents loved his story and were thrilled that he'd created it. They asked him if he'd like to take his ideas a step further and think about more consequences of Bucky's butting in. Nicholas agreed. "Suppose," his mom said, "Craig and Michael still didn't want to play with Bucky. What else might happen if Bucky keeps butting in?"

This was a difficult question and Nicholas had to think hard. Finally, he remembered the title he gave his story and laughed.

> *Nicholas*: The kids will tease him, and chant, "Bucky Butt-er-in-er, Bucky Butt-er-in-er."
> *Mom*: And what else?

Nicholas: They might make up things he did and tell the
teacher.
Mom: So is it a good idea to butt in or not a good idea?
Nicholas: Not a good idea.

All three children had made substantial progress. But were
they ready to think as clearly about the consequences of actions
when they themselves were involved? And were their parents
ready to help them link how they think with how they behave
in light of those consequences? I learned that before parents
can truly comprehend the benefits of helping children think
about potential consequences, I had to first find out what parents valued.

Talking with Parents about Consequences

As I mentioned in the previous chapter, parents who want their
kids to clean their rooms often resort to the Power Approach
because this method "works." When I asked them to explain
further, they said, "The room stays neat for the next week," or
"He knows that there are consequences for being sloppy."

I told parents about a sixth-grade girl who liked to steal other
children's supplies and was told that she had to stop stealing
because she'd get in major trouble. She did indeed stop stealing, because she didn't want to "get caught." Her parents and
teacher were delighted. I was not.

Of course, not stealing is better than stealing. But I mentioned to our parents that the girl's teacher and parents were
focusing on only half of this girl's problem. Sure, she could be
convinced to stop stealing, but her reason—so she wouldn't get
caught—displayed a complete lack of empathy. She showed no
concern for her victim. And I have to conclude that if she could

figure out a way to steal without getting caught, she might well resume stealing.

Once I was in a fast-food restaurant in a train station buying a hamburger, and for a split second, I stupidly left my wallet on the counter as I turned around to get some catsup. Needless to say, my wallet was gone by the time I turned back. Had the thief thought about me? Did he stop for a second to wonder how I'd feel, how I'd get home? No, because he was simply thinking about what *he* wanted, and perhaps how to get it without being caught.

The only lasting motivation that prevents us from hurting others emotionally or physically is that we don't *want* to hurt them. This feeling must emanate from a place very deep within us. Those who lack this feeling, who cannot think about the pain they are incurring, will stop at nothing if they think they have a shot at not getting caught.

In other words, those strategies that focus on "what's expected"—whether they are used to get a child to stop stealing, or to clean her room—are shortsighted. They only work in the here and now, not in the future. We want kids to be able to make decisions whose consequences are clear to them not just in the moment but in the days and weeks and years to come.

When children are able and then free to think of solutions to problems in light of what might happen next, taking into consideration their own and others' feelings, they feel empowered. They are proud that the ideas arose within them, belong to them. And they're much more likely to carry out their ideas than those demanded, explained, or even suggested by us.

How can parents who are used to demanding, explaining, and suggesting shift to the Problem-Solving Approach? Just keep one simple sentence in mind, and you will find letting your child think for himself much easier: *Turn a statement into a question.*

In Real Life

Problems with Other Children

Sarah, as we have seen, has started to be able to think of solutions and add consequences in fictitious situations. She still needs time, however, to apply these lessons when real problems arise. But kids aren't the only ones who have trouble using ICPS in real life. Some parents, especially those learning the Problem-Solving Approach for the first time, are also inclined to resort to other approaches in the heat of the moment, especially when they are feeling exasperated.

Here's what happened when Sarah had a bad day at school.

> *Dad*: Sarah, your teacher tells us you're bullying kids again and disrupting the class. If you keep this up, you won't learn anything and you won't have any friends!
>
> *Sarah*: I don't care!
>
> *Dad*: You're old enough to know better. If you don't stop that bullying I'm going to have to ground you until you do care!

Later, when I spoke to Sarah's dad, he was upset that he'd forgotten everything he knew about the Problem-Solving Approach. But just as we teach children not to give up too soon, I told Sarah's dad not to despair. It's just as difficult for parents to learn new behavior—how to talk to their children using ICPS dialogues, for example—as it is for children to learn to change how they act. Sarah's dad simply needed a little more patience, with himself and his daughter. After we reviewed the Problem-Solving Approach, Sarah's dad tried again:

Dad (*in a non-threatening tone*): Why do you have a need
   to bully other kids?
Sarah: I don't know.
Dad: If you think really hard, I know you can think of a
   reason.
Sarah: Dad, no one likes me.
Dad: Is bullying the kids a way to get them to like you?
Sarah: I guess not.
Dad: What happens when you bully them?
Sarah: They tell the teacher and I get in trouble.
Dad: And what else happens?
Sarah: They all run away.
Dad: And how do you feel about that?
Sarah: Sad.
Dad: And how do you think they feel when you bully
   them?
Sarah: Scared—and hurt.
Dad: How do you feel when they're scared, and hurt?
Sarah: Sad.
Dad: What can you do so they won't feel scared and hurt
   and you won't feel sad?
Sarah: Be their friend.

When asked to think about what happens after she bullies her
classmates, Sarah's first thought was that she'd get in trouble—an
external consequence. What Sarah is beginning to understand,
with her father's guidance, is that actions have "internal" consequences—those of a more empathic nature—that reflect how she
might feel if she hurts others. A child who stops hitting other children because he genuinely doesn't want to hurt others will be less
likely to revert to his old behavior than one who experiences a
quick over-and-done-with punishment.

This is why, as I described in Chapter 3, it is so important for
children to care about their own feelings before they can care

about others'. Now, thanks to ICPS, Sarah is beginning to do that. I once worked with a girl who used to be a bully before her parents began the ICPS method at home. After learning to problem solve, the girl told her mother that she stopped bullying others not because she was threatened with suspension or with being grounded, but because "It hurts me inside. I was just showing off for my friends."

Nicholas had practice sharpening his consequential thinking skills the day he thought that Raymond stole his pencil at school.

Mom: Why do you think that?

Nicholas: 'Cause it fell out of my pocket and he was using it.

Mom: Then what happened?

Nicholas: I told him I would never let him use my things, ever!

Mom: What did Raymond do or say?

Nicholas: Nothing.

Mom: Are you and Raymond friends?

Nicholas: Not anymore.

Mom: Is that what you want?

Nicholas: I guess not.

Mom: What else could happen if you talk to Raymond like that?

Nicholas: He won't let me use his things either.

Mom: And how would you feel about that?

Nicholas: Sad.

Mom: What else could you say to Raymond when you saw him with your pencil?

Nicholas: That's my pencil and I need it.

The next day, Nicholas apologized for yelling at Raymond, even though he was still hurt to think that someone would do to him what he'd never think to do to anyone else. But he learned something he could not have learned when he was accusing Raymond of stealing: He learned that Raymond did not know the pencil was Nicholas's and did not think he stole it. Nicholas realized that not talking with Raymond first, and not listening to what he had to say, could have cost him a good friend.

To help Donna, who still preferred to write in her diary, I suggested that her mom create a sheet that children like to fill out when their teachers do the "I Can Problem Solve" (ICPS) program at school. We called the sheet "Did I ICPS Today?" as displayed at the end of this chapter. You can make a sheet for your child, and duplicate it on colored paper. Donna, for example, likes to call these pages "the yellow sheets."

Donna enjoyed filling out her "yellow sheets," and made them part of her diary. Sometimes she would observe a problem at school between two or more of her classmates, and write in her diary how she thought they might have felt and what they could do to solve the problem. Even though she couldn't always think of five solutions to a problem called for on the sheet, this activity not only made her more aware of others, but got her thinking about what she would do if she encountered a problem of her own.

One day she felt a need to help another in distress—her classmate Wendy who was being teased for being fat. She told the teaser to stop because, "Wendy can't help it and people feel hurt when you do that." The girl who was teasing Wendy was so surprised to hear Donna speak up that she not only stopped, but it wasn't long before all three became best friends. Donna was thrilled about this.

Donna liked filling out her "yellow sheets" so much that I showed them to all the parents I was working with, including Sarah's and Nicholas's.

Soon after Sarah had begun keeping her yellow sheets, a boy at school called her "stupid" for getting a low grade on a test. At first, Sarah lashed out at him, but then she did something different. Turning to her yellow sheet, she wrote that she felt angry and that he probably felt "smug." She also wrote that she called him stupid in return, and that she could have gotten him into trouble by telling the teacher he had cheated. But she also recognized that neither of those solutions would win the boy over. After she thought for a long time, she wrote, "I could have told him, 'I wouldn't say that to you if you got a low grade.'" Then she got very excited and wrote a poem on her sheet:

> *Steven made me mad today.*
> *I scared him and now he's a mess.*
> *Now I'm sorry for what I did.*
> *I forgot my ICPS.*

Eight-year-old Sheryl, who was being mercilessly teased for being fat wanted nothing more than to give her tormenter a good, swift kick. But remembering *her* ICPS, she turned to the girl and quietly said, "I'm built differently from you."

Often, children this age also clash with friends. A very common problem arises between good friends over a third party. Sylvie and Francine, both age twelve, were planning a party. Sylvie wanted to invite her friend Annie, but Francine didn't want Annie to come. Francine explained that she didn't get along with Annie, and that she'd be uncomfortable if Annie were there. Francine's mom talked with her about this:

Mom: How do you think the girl will feel being left out?
Francine: Sad.
Mom: How do you think Sylvie will feel if you give her a hard time about this?
Francine: Mad.
Mom: Why don't you talk this over with Sylvie and maybe you two can solve it together.
   (*Francine decided to invite Sylvie over to her house.*)

Francine: I'd really feel uncomfortable if Annie comes to
the party 'cause we don't get along.
Sylvie: Couldn't you just stay away from her?
Francine: It would be hard. It's a small party.
Sylvie: Well it's my house and she's my friend and I don't
want to lose her.

That comment stuck with Francine. She realized that if she
insisted on Annie not coming, she might lose Sylvie's friendship.

Francine: Okay. I'll just try to stay away from her.

Francine learned a very important lesson. She realized that
she had to include Sylvie's feelings in the equation, not just her
own. Because she didn't want to lose her friend, she was able to
relegate Annie's coming to the party as secondary.

Thinking of a consequence to a solution is a step ahead of
thinking of a solution alone. But children must not stop there.
For Francine, thinking that she might lose Sylvie's friendship by
insisting that the other girl not attend the party was the first step
toward resolving the problem. But simply succumbing to Sylvie's
wishes would not have helped Francine to feel better either. It
was when she thought of another satisfying solution that the
problem was solved.

Problems between Siblings

Nicholas's sister, Tara, was starting to become even more of a
pest in his eyes. Although she'd gotten better about wanting to
play with him and his friends, she still wanted to use his things. If
he got a model airplane for his birthday, she wanted to play with
it. He didn't mind sharing his things up to a point, but it began
to seem as if Tara didn't even want her own things, only those
belonging to her brother. Though his parents tried to explain

that this was only a phase that would pass, Nicholas was still upset, perhaps understandably so. One day, when Tara took Nicholas's bike, even though she had one of her own, I urged his parents to think about how they could use the Problem-Solving Approach to handle this situation. They talked with Nicholas, out of earshot of Tara.

Mom: Can you think about why Tara might have taken your bike?

Nicholas: She told me she wishes she was a boy.

Dad: Oh, you didn't tell me that.

Nicholas: I thought it was stupid.

Dad: And what did you do?

Nicholas: I just told her never to do that again.

Dad: And how do you think she felt when you said that?

Nicholas: Bad, but I was mad.

Mom: I understand that you feel your belongings are yours. Can you think of a way to solve this problem so she doesn't feel bad, and you can still feel good?

Nicholas: I guess I could tell her to ask me when she wants to borrow something of mine, and I'll decide if she can have it.

Mom: And then what might happen?

Nicholas: She might not ask and then I'll be more mad.

Mom: That might happen. Can you think of a way to talk to her so that won't happen?

Nicholas: I could tell her that if she asks, I would probably let her have it, and then tell her when I want it back.

As I discussed in Chapter 5, understanding why people do what they do may open up new solutions to solve a problem. In this case, Nicholas was helped to understand Tara's underlying motives and to think beyond her peskiness. Indeed, when he made his possessions more available, Tara felt less of a need to pester.

If you have a daughter who has an older brother, you may encounter similar problems in your home too. It is not uncommon for a younger girl to want to be like her older brother, even idolize him. The more you try to ignore your daughter's feelings, or urge her to play with her own friends and belongings, the more her needs may be heightened. For most girls, this is a phase that *will* pass. But you can cut down on household tensions while it lasts by using the Problem-Solving Approach with your daughter and your son.

Problems between Parent and Child

Consequences are also important to think about when problems come up between children and their parents. Remember the problem that Nicholas had with his father when he forgot to rake leaves, as discussed in Chapter 6? Their initial discussion, after which Nicholas generated some ideas to help him remember to do his chore, helped them get beyond anger and frustration. The next time the subject came up, he and his father had an important conversation about this.

Nicholas's dad started the conversation by talking about feelings.

> *Dad*: How do you think I feel when you forget to rake the leaves?
>
> *Nicholas*: Mad.
>
> *Dad*: We've talked about other ways people can feel too. How else do you think I might feel about this?
>
> *Nicholas*: Maybe disappointed, frustrated?

One of the remarkable features of the Problem-Solving Approach is that not only do we come to understand how our kids feel, but we may better understand how we feel. When Nicholas answered "disappointed and frustrated," his dad thought for a moment and recognized that his feelings went beyond that. He realized that he also felt hurt, and that he was experiencing a loss of trust in his son—a consequence his son could not have imagined. It was critical to Nicholas's dad that his son know these feelings. He decided to combine the Problem-Solving Approach with the Explaining Approach.

> *Dad*: Yes, I do I feel disappointed and frustrated. I also feel hurt. I feel as if I can't count on you to do something when I ask you to.
>
> *Nicholas*: I didn't think of that. I really do forget. I'll try the ideas I thought of before and I'll really try to remember.

Sometimes, solving the problem at hand depends on having your child understand your feelings. Since there's no way for your child to know your perspective, you need to explain it to him. However, it is also vital that you use this explanation as a springboard for solving the rest of the problem.

This conversation was as important for Nicholas's dad as it was for Nicholas—both learned about the feelings of the other person. Nicholas now had a new reason to follow through on his own solutions, mentioned in Chapter 6. He really didn't want to let his dad down anymore.

For his part, Nicholas's dad told me that he understood his own feelings for the first time. "After we had our ICPS talk," he told me, "it changed our relationship. I trust him more and he trusts me. It's not that he never forgets his responsibilities around here—he's still just a kid. But when he does, I don't blow up. We talk about it."

Eventually, Nicholas learned to take better responsibility for the leaves, Sarah learned to clean her room, and Charise learned to help with the dishes. These are excellent examples of how the Problem-Solving Approach does not mean letting children do whatever they want, but rather, helps them to become responsible members of the family in ways that empower everyone.

How could this approach help a mother whose ten-year-old daughter stole all the money from her wallet? This mom wanted to say something like, "You stole my money! Don't you know right from wrong by now? You're grounded for a month!" But after she was versed in the ICPS method, she took a very different approach.

> *Mom (in a non-threatening tone of voice)*: Why didn't you ask me for money if you needed it?
> *Child*: I knew you'd say no and I needed it.
> *Mom*: Why did you need it?
> *Child*: I needed it for a present for my friend.
> *Mom*: What do you think could happen if you take all my money?
> *Child*: You'd ground me.
> *Mom*: I might do that. What do you think could happen to me?
> *Child*: Oh, you might need it and not have it.
> *Mom*: How do you think I feel about this now?
> *Child*: Sad.
> *Mom*: And how else do you think I might feel?
> *Child*: Disappointed.
> *Mom*: And how do you feel now?
> *Child*: I'm sorry, Mom. I won't do it again.
> *Mom*: What are you going to do next time you need more money?
> *Child*: I'll ask you.
> *Mom*: And when you know you'll need more money, what

can you do with your allowance so you'll have enough
when you need it?
Child: Save it.

Although this mother did make her child save her allowance
to pay her back, a realistic and reasonable request, this dialogue
accomplished many goals. The girl was helped to think what
might happen to her beyond "getting grounded"—which, no
matter how odious, would remain an external consequence,
something that was imposed upon her. Instead, the girl was
given the opportunity to think about how her actions would
affect another person ("You might need [money] and not
have it"), and how her actions would affect how she herself
may feel.

If her parents want to prevent this girl from stealing again,
they have to nurture this sense of empathy from within. Not only
will she learn right from wrong, but this talk will cast a long
shadow. It will resonate much longer than the fear of getting
caught and being punished. Now, this girl doesn't *want* to hurt
others. And she will also be able to think about how else to meet
her needs without hurting others in the process.

Parents also get very angry when their children do things that
go against their wishes. Carla's mother, for example, assumed
that her eleven-year-old daughter wore her hair up in a "trashy"
style to be intentionally defiant and disrespectful. Mom tried to
assert her authority, saying, "I won't have you looking this way!"
But her orders fell on deaf ears. She was afraid that next her
daughter would come home with various body parts pierced.
That's when she decided to talk to Carla in a different way:

Mom: I don't like my eleven-year-old looking like fifteen.
 Why do you need to comb your hair this way?
Carla: 'Cause all my friends are doing it.

Mom: I would like to be involved in how you look. Otherwise, I feel as if I'm shut out of your life.
Carla: Can we both be involved in how I look?
Mom: What do you mean?
Carla: Some days I'll wear my hair up and some days I won't.
Mom: That sounds reasonable. Let's try that.

Like Nicholas's father, Carla's mom combined the Explaining Approach with the Problem-Solving Approach; that is, she explained why she felt the way she did. This enabled Carla to come up with a solution that both could accept. In addition, Carla felt that her mom respected her when her mom didn't shut out her solution. I asked Carla's mom how she felt when she talked with her daughter this way, and looking very pleased, she said, "For the first time I don't feel so ignored. And we solved a problem that we've been battling on a regular basis. I wish we had talked about this a long time ago."

Problems around quirky dress or fancy hairdos are not unusual for children Carla's age, and if dealt with quickly and quietly, they generally pass rather quickly. Perhaps it is best to let children experiment within reasonable limits, use the Problem-Solving Approach as needed, and then trust them.

Problems between Teacher and Child

Quite often children are unable to resolve problems that come up with their teachers because they are afraid of the consequences that may ensue. Teachers, after all, have a lot of authority, and children are well aware of their own lack of power.

Just as Donna was learning to become a little more assertive with her peers, a problem arose with her teacher. This was the first time Donna had encountered such a situation, and as a result her mom was a little slow in starting to ICPS.

Donna: Mom, the teacher said I was cheating.
Mom: Were you?
Donna: No. Honest. No.
Mom: Then you should go tell the teacher.
Donna: I can't. She'll say I shouldn't back-talk her.

Donna's mom tried to direct Donna to tell the teacher instead of telling the teacher herself, at least until Donna said she couldn't. But she was still suggesting what Donna should do, thereby still doing the thinking for her.

I talked to her about how she could use ICPS in this situation. Donna's mom then began this conversation:

Mom: What can you do now?
Donna: I can't tell the teacher. She'll think I'm talking back.
Mom: This is a tough one. Think real hard. What else can you do?

Donna could not think of a solution. This is not uncommon. There will be times when your child won't be able to think of something to do or say, and you will be tempted to help them by voicing a suggestion. Unless your child is going to get hurt or into a dangerous situation, just be patient and say, "I know you can think of something. Take your time." Firmly resist the impulse to think for your child. In a day or two, she may well come up with her own solution.

Sure enough, the next day Donna thought of something she could do.

Donna: I can ask her how I can prove to her that I didn't cheat.
Mom: That might help. Go ahead and try that.

Donna came home after school beaming. "Mom," she said, "Mrs. Sawyer said she'd put me off to the side on the next test. I know she'll see I didn't cheat." When you have a conversation like this, carefully note how proud your child looks and sounds. Recalling this pride will help you resolve to avoid revealing your thoughts the next time a situation arises, and allow your child to figure her way out of an enigma.

Sarah had a different problem. She felt she was being treated unfairly by her teacher because she was never called on to be class messenger, delivering messages to the nurse and main office. Her mom, who now felt very comfortable with ICPS dialoguing, talked with her like this:

> *Mom*: Do you know why you don't get picked to be messenger?
> *Sarah*: No. It's not fair.
> *Mom*: What happened last time she sent you with a message to take somewhere?
> *Sarah*: I guess I messed around in the halls.
> *Mom*: How do you think your teacher felt about that?
> *Sarah*: Mad.
> *Mom*: And what else might your teacher think?
> *Sarah*: I don't know.
> *Mom*: If she needs a message delivered, what does she think might happen if she picks you?
> *Sarah*: It won't get there.
> *Mom*: What can you say to her now?
> *Sarah*: You can trust me. Please give me another chance.
> *Mom*: Good thinking. Go ahead and try that.

Sarah tried this tack, but her teacher was not ready to grant Sarah so much responsibility. Her mom continued the dialogue.

> *Mom*: I'm glad you tried. Try to think of something different you can say or do.

Sarah: Next time she asks me to do something, I'll do it and not complain.

This problem was not solved so readily, because it took time for Sarah to gain her teacher's trust. But being chosen messenger was important to her, and she worked very hard, as she later put it, "to make her teacher proud." When she finally was chosen, she made sure she behaved responsibly. This was one more step on her road to social and emotional competence.

Nicholas came home upset one day because his teacher yelled at him for chewing gum in class. While it would be ideal if all adults dialogued with children, including those at school, Nicholas's mom told him, "Not everyone is an ICPSer. You have to use your ICPS skills even with people who don't."

Mom: Why do you think she has that rule?

Nicholas: 'Cause it bothers her?

Mom: That's one possible reason. Can you think of another?

Nicholas: Then she'd have to let everybody do it?

Mom: What would it sound like if everyone chewed gum at the same time?

Nicholas: Yeah, I see.

Mom: Is it fair for you to chew gum and not the others?

This short dialogue helped Nicholas understand that there was a reason for this rule, and to appreciate the consequences if gum chewing were allowed.

Donna's newfound assertiveness, and Sarah's emerging problem-solving skills may seem to have appeared rather suddenly. They didn't. It took four months of practice for both girls to learn the ICPS skills described so far. But they still had one more problem-solving skill to learn—how to plan ahead and appreciate that sometimes it takes time to reach a goal.

Summing Up

- Help your child develop empathy by:
  1. Encouraging him to think beyond "external" consequences that are over and done with quickly, such as being grounded or having his allowance taken away for a week.
  2. Guiding him to think about how what he does or says affects another either physically ("I hurt him") or emotionally ("I hurt his feelings").
  3. Asking him how he feels inside if he hurts someone physically or emotionally.

- Help your child think of consequences to what she does or says in addition to how she and others feel—consequences that may be either positive or negative.

- Ask your child to evaluate for himself whether his idea is or is not a good one in light of potential consequences. If his idea is not a good one, ask him to think of a different way to solve the problem.

- When you let children solve their own problems by turning a statement into a question, you're sending an important message: I trust you to make good decisions, and I respect how you think and feel about things.

DID I ICPS TODAY?

The problem was _____.

Who was involved? _____ and _____.

Before the problem was solved, I felt _____ and _____.

The other(s) probably felt _____ and _____.

My solution was _____

_____.

What happened next (the consequence) was _____

_____.

Was the problem solved? _____.

If the problem was not solved, five others things I could have said or done are:

1.

2.

3.

4.

5.

Which one might be the best solution of all?

Why might that be the best one?

Some things I might think about the next time a problem comes up are:

_____

_____

◀ 8 ▶

What's My Plan?

Kids who can take control of their lives will not let life take control of them.

Many problems that come up between people can be solved with a single solution. If a child can't follow the directions to make a model sailboat by herself, she could "ask someone to help," and if that doesn't work, she could try a new approach, such as "explain why she needs help." A child who wants to make new friends can come up with a series of single, unconnected solutions, such as "going to visit the boy next door," "having a party," or "meeting them at school." In Chapter 6, Sarah realized it would be more satisfying to ask JoAnn for the magic marker than to intimidate her, because the first solution would have fewer potentially painful consequences.

But sometimes solving a problem between people is not so simple. Sometimes it requires a different, more complex skill, called means-ends thinking, or sequenced planning. At around age eight, this skill begins to distinguish more competent problem solvers from those who are less skilled. Children need a combination of skills to be good at sequenced planning. Specifically, they need to be able to think about:

- What steps can I take to reach my goal? What do I do first, second, etc?
- What obstacles might interfere on the way toward my goal?
- Do I have a realistic alternative idea if the object is insurmountable?
- When is the best time to try my plan?
- How long will it take to complete my plan?

To make a new friend, for example, a child skilled in sequenced planning might resort to a more sophisticated process of thought than focusing on one, isolated solution at a time. Instead of thinking, "She should give her something," and then think of a separate, new solution, such as, "Have a party," Lauren, age nine, thought of a sequence of events. That sequence included a potential obstacle—"She won't like what I give her." She then thought of a way around that obstacle: "I could find out what she likes," and then decided on a good time to do that: "I'll buy it for her birthday."

In other words, to enact a sequenced plan, a child needs to be able to put his plan into action, recognize that problem solving is not always smooth sailing, and evaluate the timing of his act. Clearly, it is a more demanding task than is alternative solution thinking, where the sole requirement is to identify a single type or category of solution.

Building Skills for Sequenced Planning

There are several steps toward mastering sequenced planning, but the very first is to help your child determine his real goal. For example, if the goal is to buy candy for a party that evening, a child has to focus on getting the candy in time for the party, not just getting candy. Any obstacles that could interfere must be anticipated and circumvented. If your child waits until the end of the day to shop, he risks showing up after the store has closed. Then he would have to change his plan, which may entail traveling to another store that is open but farther away. Would he still be able to make the party in time?

Because of the complexity of sequenced planning, it is helpful to break it into its separate parts when first presenting exercises to help your child learn this skill.

Steps Toward the Goal

You can help your child think of sequenced steps by starting with a very simple example. You can say, "Belinda wants to grow a garden. What's the first thing she has to do?" One child said she has to plant the seeds, and her mom asked, "What does she have to do even before that? What is step one?" The child answered, "She has to buy them first." "Okay," said her mom. "First she has to buy them, then she plants them. Then what? What's step three?" Let your child make up a goal and tell you step 1, step 2, etc. You can use this exercise to go in the other direction; for example, you can ask what Belinda has to do before she buys the seeds, and where she would get the money for them.

This exercise helps children envision how many steps are involved in the movement toward achieving any goal.

What Obstacles Might Get in the Way?

Children also need to realize that even the most thoughtful plans encounter unexpected roadblocks. Good planners know how to either remove the obstacles or go around them. You can help your child think about obstacles to reaching a plan by making it fun. Introduce silly, or impossible, scenarios by playing the "I Want to But . . ." game. You can say:

> I want to ride in a car from New York to London,
>   but . . .
> I want to climb a mountain, but . . .
> Alexander Graham Bell wanted to tell Bill Gates how he
>   invented the telephone, but . . .
> I want to be the next Michael Jordan, but . . .
> I want to enjoy a movie when I'm in France, but . . .
> I want to sing with the Back Street Boys, but . . .

Some of these examples have several possible obstacles, such as being too short to be the next Michael Jordan, or not having enough talent. I can't sing with the Back Street Boys because I have laryngitis, or because I'm a girl. I can't climb a mountain because I have no rope, or because I'm scared. It doesn't matter what your child says as long as it presents a logical obstacle to reaching the goal. Let your child make up some scenarios too.

Timing of Acts

To learn to think about the timing of taking an action, children ages eight to twelve love the "Good-Time or Not-Good-Time" game. By age eight, children can begin to think about how timing of an act is part of a larger plan, such as how timing an act fits into a sequence of steps and helps to avoid potential obstacles. Waiting for a friend's birthday to give her something she likes, as Lauren suggested, was part of that larger plan.

You can start out by offering funny, even very silly examples of not-good times, mixing them with examples that are good times. You can say, "Tell me if it is or is not a good time for these people to act."

- Laury asks her sister to borrow her sweater—right after she broke her sister's favorite glass horse.
- George asks his dad to shoot baskets with him—just after his dad broke his leg.
- Jolene asks her teacher something—after her teacher finished talking to someone at the door.
- Ramona asks her brother to help her with her homework—while he's floating down from an airplane in a parachute.
- Fred tells his dad he'd like a new camera—a week before his birthday.
- Faith won an award for her poem and calls her friend to tell her about it—at four o'clock in the morning.
- Jill put her pencil down—right after the teacher said the test was over.
- Luke asks his friend for a favor—right after his friend was yelled at by his teacher.
- Michelle turned off her computer—ten minutes after Mom called everyone for dinner.
- Russell throws a ball to his teammate—right after the coach said, "play ball."
- Marion shouted out an answer to a question in class—right after the teacher called on someone else.

Let your child make up silly and not-silly examples of her own. Ask her to include some things people do at good times and not-good times. For example, when Donna was asked to think of a not-good time for Belinda to water the garden, she said, "After the plants have died." Then she added, "And a good time would be before they dry out and die." Later, the game helped Donna in real life. Needing help with an art project, Donna asked her mother—but did so right after her mom found out a friend had died and was feeling very sad. When her mom didn't respond, Donna was able to recognize her mother's sadness, and waited until she was in a better mood.

This game also helped Sarah in her real life. Seeing two friends playing checkers, she wanted to join them. In the past, she would have barged in on them in the middle of their game. Now, she checked her inclination to behave in an "I can't wait" mode, paused, and waited until their game was finished before asking if she could play too.

Thinking about timing is not easy. I fall into this trap myself. Just recently, I wanted to play tennis with a particular person, and as soon as I saw her I asked her to play. Even though I knew she had just played because she was walking off the court, I didn't really notice that she was hot and tired. When she said, "No thanks," I could have concluded that she didn't want to play with me. But I realized that I picked a not-good time to ask her, which helped me avoid drawing a false assumption.

How Long Will It Take?

Planning steps to reach a goal involves recognizing that we can't always have what we want the minute we want it. Rarely do we meet somebody—or even do something with that person after a first meeting, like have a cup of coffee—and conclude that we are friends. It takes time, sometimes a long time, to make a friend. Children who can think in ways that are not impulsive, who appreciate that things can take time, are less likely to behave in ways that are not impulsive. Their plan takes into account the fact that it may take some time for them to accomplish their goal. Nicholas, for example, created a fictitious character named Stuart, who wanted to make the travel soccer team. He described how Stuart reserved one hour every day for practice, and in three months was good enough to get on the team. This is a good example of nonimpulsive thinking by a child who does not act impulsively in real life.

The ability to think about time and timing is important. Research indicates that children who behave in impulsive ways are much more likely to think events will occur sooner than children who do not behave that way. In other words, they have a less realistic understanding of the amount of time needed to accomplish a goal. Sarah, for example, thought she could have a whole new wardrobe the day after she decided that might help her make friends at school. Perhaps she also assumed that all she needed to do was show up at school in her new clothes and her classmates would be so impressed that they'd immediately treat her differently. For her part, Donna thought it would only take a few days for a plant to grow from a seed. It's no wonder that children like Donna and Sarah are likely to wait until the last day to start a two-week project for school, and then be shocked to discover that they can't get it done in time.

Beginning at age eight, most children can understand the concept that we approach goals through a series of steps, that obstacles may arise, and that there are good and not-good times to ask for what you want. However, it is often not until about age ten that youngsters can realistically think about how long things might take. For eight- and nine-year-olds who are not able to think about how the passage of time affects what can be accomplished, just focus on the other elements of sequenced planning for now.

Putting the Parts Together

Parents I worked with began helping their children create sequenced plans by using the following story. They told their children, "This year the school decided that every class would have a class president, and Adrian wanted the class to pick her.

The story ends up with Adrian being picked class president. This story has a beginning and an ending, but no middle. You're going to make up the middle. I want to see everything happen, just like in a movie. I don't want to miss anything. Make sure your story has steps toward the goal, at least one obstacle that gets in the way, and tell how long you think it might take to carry out a step or to reach a goal. If you can, include a good time to carry out a step."

Methodically verbalizing the word "steps" helped Sarah learn this new skill. Her story went like this:

> The teacher said, "We need a new class president," and Adrian and Paulette both wanted the job the most. When they voted, half the class picked Adrian and half picked Paulette. It was a tie. *Step #1*: Each girl wrote a speech. Adrian told everyone she would give them promises if they elected her. But they didn't believe her. *Step #2*: She wanted to talk to Tina, the most popular girl, and Tina could get her friends to vote for her. But Tina was sick. *Step #3*: So Adrian went up and talked again, and the class clapped louder and she said, "One more thing, I can help you if you have problems to solve." Paulette couldn't compete with her. The class elected Adrian as the new class president.

Although she didn't specifically verbalize the word "obstacle," Sarah was able to think of several of them. She began her story by uncovering an obstacle—the tie vote. The first step of her plan was for Adrian to tell her classmates she would "give them promises." But she recognized a potential obstacle to that step—"they didn't believe her." Sarah then had to change her plan. Her next step, her hope that Tina, the most popular girl, could help her get votes also met with an obstacle—Tina was sick. Adrian got around that obstacle by adding another incentive—

offering to help her classmates with their problems. Sarah dismissed Paulette by giving her no strategies, and that's how Adrian was elected class president.

Because Sarah did not add the element of time or timing on her own, her mom added one more question: "How long do you think it took Adrian to create her plan?" Sarah thought about that and said, "It took her two hours to write her speech."

What a change from Sarah's more impulsive thinking style that she relied on before her parents started ICPS.

Donna had more difficulty with this task. As she did before ICPS, she still focused on what happened after the goal was reached:

> Adrian told the kids in her class that they should choose
> her president 'cause she's nice and 'cause she likes them.
> They picked her president and she was so glad, she threw
> a little party for them for voting for her. They had a lot of
> fun and Adrian was very happy.

To help Donna focus on *how* to reach a goal, I told Donna's mom to ask her, "What is the first thing Adrian did when she decided she wanted to be picked class president?" Donna repeated that she told them to choose her 'cause she's nice and 'cause she likes them. Her mom then asked, "Is it always that easy to get what you want? What might the kids in her class do or say if Adrian says that?"

"Okay," answered Donna.

"They might say okay. What else might they say? Do you remember our 'I Want to But . . .' game? Think of something they might say that would make her have to change her plan."

"They might say, 'But we don't like you,'" said Donna.

"Okay. What's the next step she can take to get around that obstacle?"

"She can ask them why they don't like her and they might say 'cause she's ugly," Donna said.

"And then what?" asked Mom.

"She can make herself pretty and then they'll like her."

"And how will she do that?"

"She'll comb her hair."

Donna's mom didn't ask now about how long it would take for her to be elected president. She knew that Donna wasn't quite ready for that, and was pleased just to see her daughter so involved in her story for now.

Later that evening, Donna decided to expand this plan in her diary. She wrote about how Adrian would save her money from her allowance to buy new clothes so she would be pretty. She also added another new step—that Adrian would say that she would play with anyone who wanted to play with her. Though Donna may not have been ready to enact this plan in real life, this exercise was still very significant. In creating a plan for Adrian, she was doing all the thinking and planning herself

Now let's recall the story I described in Chapter 1, about how a fictitious character, Anita, could make friends. Sarah's initial story consisted of just one step—asking the group to play frisbee. The rest of her story was concerned with what they did after they were friends. Here's how she retold the story *after* becoming aware of the importance of *sequenced steps*:

Anita could give little presents to the kids at school but that didn't win her any friends. One day she asked one of them point blank, "Why won't you be my friend? I've done so many things for you." The girl told her she knew she was just trying to bribe her and the other kids were talking about her behind her back. Then one day she noticed one of the girls was having trouble with her homework so she offered to help. After a week, the girl got an A on her test. She was so grateful, they became friends.

In the first version, Sarah moved right to the goal without considering obstacles or time. Now Sarah had a plan. And when her character encountered her first obstacle, she was able to change her plan. True, Sarah didn't reach the goal of making more than one friend, but she created a plan that incorporated all of the three skills comprised in sequenced planning.

Donna's only step in her first story about Anita, introducing herself to others, was met with an obstacle when one girl said, "I don't like you"—but she changed her mind as if by magic, with no intervention by Anita at all.

Like Sarah's, Donna's new story is quite different.

Anita goes to the neighbors' house and their eleven-year-old daughter answers the door. "Hi, my name is Anita, and I just moved in. Do you want to play?"

The girl says, "I already have friends, thank you," and closes the door. Anita walks away and doesn't want to make new friends.

The next day she goes to school and the teacher introduces her to the class. Everyone seems like they don't care.

One day she's by a river near her house, and she's trying to collect stuff, and she hears, "Help, help!" She runs to where the screams are coming from and she sees the girl who told her she already had friends. She's in the river and she can't swim. So Anita runs and jumps in and pulls the girl out of the river. All her friends were there too but they couldn't do anything 'cause they were too scared. Anita asks her if she's okay, and the girl says, "Yes, you saved my life." She apologizes for being nasty to her, and Anita says, "That's okay. Do you want to be friends?"

The girl says, "Yes, of course," and all her other friends now think she's the greatest and she becomes very popular.

In this version, Donna recognized an obstacle to her request, and typical of Donna in real life, at first depicted Anita as giving up. But the girl was able to identify a potential liaison to the group, and waited for an opportunity to take an active step. Over time, this kind of sequenced planning helped her reach her goal.

Our ICPS kids now have a new skill to use when problems arise in their lives.

In Real Life

Donna's mom used her daughter's new sequenced planning plans in fictitious situations to help her overcome her fears of approaching classmates during recess.

> *Mom*: Tell me what's on your mind when kids are jumping rope on the playground.
> *Donna*: I want to jump too.
> *Mom*: And then what do you do?
> *Donna*: I watch them.
> *Mom*: And then what?
> *Donna*: Nothing, I just watch them.
> *Mom*: What do you want to happen?
> *Donna*: I wish they'd ask me to jump.
> *Mom*: What can you do so they might ask you to jump?
> *Donna*: I could ask them but they'd probably say no.
> (*Here, Donna gives voice to her fear of rejection.*)
> *Mom*: Okay. That's a possible obstacle. Remember our "I Want to But . . ." game? You want to ask them *but*

you're afraid they might say no. What can you do
next? What will be your next step?

Donna: I don't know.

Mom: What do you enjoy doing?

Donna (remembering her creative gingerbread man): I like
to make funny cookies.

Mom: How could you use that to solve your problem?

Donna: I could tell one of them what I did and ask if
she'd like to make a funny cookie with me.

Mom: And when's a good time to do that?

Donna: At lunchtime. When she's hungry.

Mom: You're thinking about this very well now. If you
ask and the girl says no, imagine what you might
do or say next so you end up making a funny cookie
together.

Donna: I could make another cookie at home and show it
to her.

Donna proudly followed through on her strategy, and one of
the girls showed interest in making cookies with her. Despite this
connection, however, Donna still was afraid to approach the
group of jump-ropers at recess. Again, her mom used the ICPS
method to give Donna hints without telling her what to do.

Mom: Now that you know Rita better, and she still jumps
rope at recess, what can you do next so that you can
jump rope with her and the other girls?

Donna: I could ask Rita if I could jump rope with them. If
she tells them to let me play, they'll say yes.

Mom: Okay, and when is a good time to ask her?

Donna: When we're making our funny cookies.

Mom: Good thinking. You're getting to be a very good
problem solver.

That's what Donna did. She asked Rita to ask the other girls if she could play, easing into the situation with only one girl. Finally, she felt more comfortable taking the initiative to join her peers. Had her mother *suggested* the same steps toward the goal that her daughter ultimately thought of herself, Donna might never have made the attempt.

Sequenced planning skills also work very well with children who wait too long to begin their homework. Although Nicholas was a good student, he often spent his afternoons playing with friends and participating in extracurricular activities. With bedtime near and his homework not done, Nicholas's parents tried explaining why he should do his homework earlier, suggested ways to schedule his time, and imposed half-hour limits on his access to the Internet and TV. Still, the problem wasn't solved. Nicholas was a good sequenced planner, but he wasn't using that skill here. This was a good opportunity for his parents to help him solve the homework crisis.

Mom: I want you to think about how you're going to plan your time so you can get everything done, including your homework.

Nicholas: I have Lacrosse practice after school and I'm home at four o'clock.

Mom: Then what will you do first when you get home?

Nicholas: I'll do my math first 'cause that's the hardest.

Mom: How long do you think that will take?

Nicholas: About forty minutes.

Mom: Okay. That will be about twenty minutes to five. Dinner is at six. What will you do then?

Nicholas: My music is due Wednesday. It's Monday now. I'll do half today and half tomorrow. If I work till five-thirty I can practice Lacrosse with Dad for a half hour.

Mom: Okay, dinner takes about an hour. Then it will be seven o'clock. What will you do then?

Nicholas: I'll practice my piano until seven-thirty. I can watch TV or go on-line with my friends till eight-thirty and then work on my science homework till nine. I'll take my shower and go to bed. Maybe I'll read my mystery for a few minutes, and then I'll fall asleep.

Mom: That's an excellent plan. You thought this through very well. Now, there's one more thing to think about. What if a friend calls and wants you to come to his house while you're doing your homework?

Nicholas: We can do it together. Or, maybe we could play and I could do my music later instead of watching TV.

Nicholas's mother asked about the possibility of a friend calling because she wanted him to think through a potential obstacle, but waited until he finished his plan so as not to interrupt his train of thought.

You might be thinking that this kind of planning is too detailed and too cumbersome. In fact, after a while, Nicholas won't have to plan the day in such detail. But to do so at first is a good way to reduce the stress he felt when faced with too much to do. Once he had his plan laid out, he could concentrate on his math homework while he was doing it without having to worry about his music homework getting done, because he knew that his schedule allotted time for music as well. Also, instead of trying to do all his music in one day, he apportioned the work over a two-day period. Now Nicholas was in control of his time instead of time controlling him. And the constant haggling with his parents about when he would do his homework subsided.

Planning my time helps me when I feel overwhelmed. Before I started practicing sequenced planning, I would sometimes feel I had so much to do that I would freeze, or go back and forth from one thing to another, and the day would go by with none of my tasks done. Now, instead of thinking about everything I have to do at once, I select one task to do later, forget about it for now, and concentrate on the task at hand. With my schedule sketched out, including every task I want to accomplish that day, I don't have to worry about getting to everything, nor do I feel guilty when I'm doing other things. And I can go to bed knowing that I did everything I could. If everything *didn't* get done, I conclude that either I had more to do than could possibly be done in one day, or that I will have to rethink my plan and set new priorities for the next day.

Sarah, like Nicholas, also had trouble starting her homework early enough so that it would be finished by bedtime. She had particular difficulty making realistic plans to complete her long-range projects, like a book report due in two weeks. Before ICPS, her dad's suggestions about when she should begin and his explanations that not doing her homework would lead to failing grades were met with resistance. Her mom would get into power plays with her by saying things like, "I told you so. When are you going to learn not to wait till the last minute to do everything!" When nothing seemed to work, she became increasingly exasperated, and even more directive, telling Sarah that she had to have the book read by a particular date, and a first draft ready three days later. Of course, this didn't help, either. One day Sarah just snapped and told her mom, "Don't tell me how to do it! I'll do it *my* way!" Sarah was old enough to comprehend how the passage of time affects what can be accomplished, and she resented being told when each item of work had to be completed. She felt as if her mother was trying to take control of her schedule, which only made her more resistant and less open to suggestions.

Although Sarah wanted to do her homework her way, she didn't have the planning skills to do that, and continued to procrastinate until it was too late. In the past, her parents would have laid down rules, such as, "No Internet and no TV until homework is done." Sarah always met these impositions by saying, "That's not fair," and moping. Now they were ready to help Sarah develop the skill of sequenced planning with the Problem-Solving Approach. By this point, Sarah was so accustomed to shutting out her parents that she wasn't able to respond at first.

Mom: How much homework do you have?
Sarah: Not that much.
Mom: How long do you think it will take?
Sarah: I don't know.
Mom: Let me see your assignments. Maybe I can help you think about this.
Sarah: I did some of it on the school bus.

Sarah's parents didn't give up. Having seen their daughter change so much in other areas, they felt confident that her resistance to planning would also subside in time. Several months later, after Sarah and her parents had more practice with this approach, the conversation went like this.

Dad: When is your report due?
Sarah: Next Thursday.
Dad: What's the first thing you have to do?
Sarah: Write my report.
Dad: What do you have to do before that?
Sarah: Read my book.
Dad: And how long do you think that will take?
Sarah: I don't know. I'll read it a little every day until I'm done.
Dad: And then what do you have to do?
Sarah: Write my report.
Dad: When do you have to start your report to have it done by next Thursday?
Sarah: Maybe on Tuesday?

Dad: Good planning. You're not going to wait until the
last minute to start your report.

Sarah now felt proud of *her* plan instead of angry and frustrated over having to listen to her mother's belittling tactics, and
her father's suggestions and explanations. Since this was the first
time Sarah talked about starting a project ahead of time, her dad
did not introduce the issues of obstacles or time.

Evan, age eleven, had a long-term project for history that
required doing research at the library because he didn't have
Internet access at home. To make a plan, he used his sequenced
planning skills, taking into account the possibility of obstacles
arising, and the necessity of considering both time (how long it
will take) and timing (when is a good time to begin each phase).
His plan included time scheduled for homework and soccer practice, which took place from three to five on Mondays, Wednes-
days, and Fridays. The first day he was given the assignment he
made an outline, with his mother's help, of what he had to do.

Mom: When is your report due?

Evan: In a week.

Mom: What do you have to do to complete your report?

Evan: I have to read the book, do some research at the
library, and write the report.

Mom: Okay. Write in your calendar when you'll do these
things.

Evan: On Monday, Tuesday, and Wednesday I'll read the
book right after dinner. I will go to the library on
Thursday right after school.

Mom: And how long do you think it will take to get what
you need from the library?

Evan: A couple of hours.

Mom: What time will you go to the library on Thursday
so you will be home in time for dinner?

Evan: Right after school.

Mom: And what day will you start writing your report?

Evan: Sunday night.

Mom: How can you plan ahead in case you end up needing more time?

Evan (*answering proudly*): I better allow more time to write my report in case I need it, so I won't have to stay up all night the night before it's due.

Mom: Good thinking, Evan. How do you feel when you make your own plan like this?

Evan: Great.

This plan is considerably more sophisticated than the one created by Sarah. Evan thought of how to plan his time around the rest of his schedule (his soccer practice), included more steps, such as going to the library, and responded to his mother's question about whether he was leaving enough time to complete his work.

Still, Sarah has come a long way from leaving everything until the last minute. She is now able to complete some tasks on time. And her mom has also found that using the Problem-Solving Approach—instead of saying things like, "I told you so; when are you going to learn not to wait till the last minute to do everything"—makes it easier for Sarah to think.

By age eleven and twelve, some children are assigned more complex, multi-part projects which teachers break into smaller parts. Martin, an ICPS-trained twelve-year-old, for example, was assigned the task of planning a trip to Nagano, Japan, the site of the 1998 Winter Olympics. In three weeks' time, he had to plan a trip with two stops along the way, create a map connecting all the stops between Philadelphia and Nagano, create a budget for the trip, choose a sporting event to attend, and report on the sport he chose. The teacher suggested deadlines for each segment of the report. With this as his anchor, and his father's help, Martin was able to use his sequenced planning skills to devote two or three days to each portion of the task, which left time for him to complete his other homework and activities as well.

Peggy, a girl in his class, felt so confident of her ICPS skills that she created her own timeline for completion instead of following the teacher's suggestions. This girl knew she'd enjoy writing about figure skating most of all, and decided to do that first. "That's how I got into the rest of the report," she explained.

The details of children's plans are not what's important. Some children begin their homework with the hardest part, as did Nicholas, others with the easiest or most enjoyable part, as Peggy did. What's important is that *they* plan, that it's their own plan, and that the plan is realistic and possible to carry out. When your child creates a plan of her own, she'll feel more in control and less stressed, and you'll feel less stressed too.

Barbara McCombs informs us that most children are not yet able to become entirely self-directed until adolescence. My colleague George Spivack found that to be the time when youngsters are able to create sophisticated sequenced plans completely on their own. With their parents' help, our ICPS kids have made important strides toward developing this skill in a way that will help prepare them for many new decisions they will have to make when they do reach those more turbulent adolescent years.

Summing Up

- Help your child define the goal so he is clear about what he is striving for.

- Help your child develop a sequenced plan, including:
  1. the first step or steps to take

2. how long the step or steps might take
3. the best time to carry out the step or steps
4. what might interfere with the goal (obstacles)
5. how the plan can be changed, if needed

Whether the goal is interpersonal (making friends), or task-oriented (completing homework), it may sometimes be necessary to change the goal if it turns out to be impossible to reach. If your child has created a viable plan and still cannot reach her goal, help her find a new, more obtainable one.

We will now look at how our ICPS kids learned to combine the skills they have been taught in a way neither they nor their parents could have imagined.

◀ 9 ▶

Advanced ICPS:
Integrating the Skills

*If relieving our emotional tension can help us to think
straight, our ability to think straight can relieve our
emotional tension.*

So far, we have explored the ways in which using specific ICPS
skills can change the way children think and behave. We've
focused on each skill independently, in order to highlight how it
works and how it propels children to act. Now it's time to put
the skills together.

In this chapter, we'll see how ICPS skills can be combined,
first two, and then three at a time, to help children solve the
problems they face.

In Fictitious Situations

More about Friendships

As we discussed earlier, negotiating friendships is particularly
important for children of this age. Children who can combine
the skills of *thinking of how people feel* with their ability to make
a *sequenced plan* often have an easier time with friends. To

encourage children to combine these two skills, our ICPS parents asked their children to create a new story about making friends that included these two skills.

Nicholas told this story about two classmates:

Paul was very angry at Ronald because Ronald didn't keep his promise to bring a video to school that he said Paul could borrow. Ronald was very worried because he wanted to be Paul's friend. He wanted to talk it out but you don't know what someone's going to do when they're really mad. So he waited until Paul cooled off and asked if he'd like to come to his house and watch it. Paul went to Ronald's house and they got to know each other better and they became friends.

Nicholas understood how both characters felt and incorporated those feelings into Ronald's plan to solve his problem. Ronald wanted to "talk it out," but foresaw an obstacle—"You don't know what someone's going to do when they're really mad." So he delayed enacting his first step—talking to Paul—until a better time. After waiting for Paul to "cool off," Ronald proceeded to the next step in his plan—inviting Paul to his house so they could get to know each other better.

Donna's new story, which she proudly wrote out in her diary, was about regaining a friend after being rejected:

Roxanne looked wistfully at her best friend, Natalie, and Natalie's new friend, Ann Marie. Ever since Natalie had met Ann Marie at the beginning of the school year, they had been playing together nonstop and completely forgetting about Roxanne. Reluctantly, Roxanne walked over to Natalie and Ann Marie, in an attempt to be noticed. Her attempt was unsuccessful. Natalie and Ann

Marie continued to play their own game of tag. "Hey, you guys," she called, "can I play?" They didn't hear her. She called out again, this time louder. Finally they noticed her and allowed her to play. But it was no use. They only chased each other as if she weren't there. Roxanne sighed and walked away.

When Natalie finally stopped playing tag, she noticed that Roxanne had left. She remembered how strange Roxanne had acted. It was as if she felt left out. She remembered how hurt her feelings had been when another friend of hers had found someone else to play with and how left out she had felt. She realized that must be how Roxanne felt.

When Natalie got home, she invited both Ann Marie and Roxanne to come over for dinner, without telling them that the other would be there. She decided that when the two girls got to know each other better, they would be good friends.

When her friends arrived, they were a little surprised to see each other, but talked a lot and discovered that they had a lot in common.

Soon they were talking like old friends. After that the three girls got along very well, and were best friends.

Donna insightfully incorporated people's feelings into her story. Though she still shows a limited understanding of how long it takes to regain an old friend or make a new one, she has mastered several other ICPS skills. By having Natalie reflect, "She remembered how hurt her feelings had been . . ." Donna is illustrating her new understanding of *empathy*. She was also able to make a *sequenced plan*.

Sarah decided to elaborate on her story about the girl running for middle school president, as related in Chapter 8:

Suzanne goes to her new school and sees a sign, "Vote for Cara Miller for Middle School President." She decides she wants to run also. She goes to the office and asks who's in charge of the elections and she goes to the teacher and tells her that she also wants to run for president. She gets a list of things she needs to do, and she has to write a speech to give on election day and make signs, and she goes home and makes five signs that say "Vote for Suzanne Thomas." She brings them in to school and is hanging one up when Cara Miller comes up to her and says, "You have no chance of beating me. I'm the most popular kid here." Then Suzanne gets upset and decides not to run, and she goes to tell the teacher who's in charge that she's dropping out. But the teacher convinces her not to quit.

The night before the election, Suzanne is nervous. She tries to write her speech. Someone she knows from school calls to say, "Good luck. I'm voting for you." That gives her confidence, and she writes in her speech that she wants to make a difference in the school, and will take suggestions and make sure they are heard. She says that everyone's ideas would be equal and that she would hear everyone's ideas. "I'll battle for us kids," she added.

When Cara gives her speech, everyone is whispering and yawning. She tells them how popular she is and that she will have a table for the cool kids and a table for the dorky kids. The dorky kids don't think that is funny and don't vote for her. So Suzanne wins and everyone likes the way she stood up for them and soon she has lots of friends.

Sarah's story shows real insight into what happens when someone does *not* consider the needs or viewpoints of others.

Coping with Bullies

Sarah's mom was pleased to see her daughter achieving this level of insight, and wanted her to apply it to other situations. Knowing that Sarah sometimes intimidated other children, she asked Sarah to write a story about bullies, and hoped that it would combine more than one of her ICPS skills. Interestingly, Sarah created a story about children who hurt others far more seriously than she ever did:

> At the end of the school day, Ann, who was eleven and in fifth grade, walked out the main door, when five of her schoolmates appeared—Lauren, Eddie, Caroline, Elizabeth, and Bill. They were known as the fifth grade bullies, and they were always beating up on kids or making fun of them. Lauren gave Ann a phony smile. "Well, well, well, it's Ann. Just who we wanted to see."
>
> Ann looked at her nervously, but reminded herself that she knew what to do if they tried to beat her up or asked her to beat someone else up. Lauren said, "We have a dare for you. We want you to beat up Candy Smith for us." Candy Smith was short, skinny, and a little bit of a dork. She was unpopular, but Ann liked her.
>
> "Unless you're too scared to," Eddie said.
>
> Ann reminded herself that there were a bunch of steps to discourage them from violence. In her head, she went over them. Step one, she thought, tell them politely but firmly that you don't want to be violent to others. "I don't want to beat up my friend," Ann told the bullies. The bullies made fun of her and made jeering remarks about how she was a chicken and a coward.
>
> Step two, she thought, don't make defensive remarks and don't lose your temper. Tell them politely that you

think what they do is wrong and ask them why they want to beat up someone who never did anything to them. When she asked them this, Elizabeth answered, "Because it's fun."

Step three, Ann thought, tell them that it's not fun for anybody else, and to consider other people's feelings. Ann said, "It's not fun for anybody else. How would you feel if someone beat you up for no reason?"

"Oh, be quiet, you little twit. You're no fun," Elizabeth said, walking away. "Come on, guys."

With that, the bullies left Ann alone and walked away.

Sarah was just as deliberate in her ability to apply *sequenced planning* skills in this story as she was in the one about making friends—perhaps because the subject matter was so close to home. Notice also that she verbalized the process she was going through by saying, "Step one," "Step two," and by thinking about what she would do before saying it out loud. She was not only able to think of *steps toward the goal*, but also included an *obstacle* with each step. Although she did not include time or timing in her story, she recognized other people's *feelings*, and also attempted to understand the *underlying motives* of the bullies. When she asked them why they wanted to beat up Candy, and had them reply, "Because it's fun," it's possible that Sarah was thinking at an extremely sophisticated level. Once, she might have thought the same way; that is, she might have attributed a superficial reason to why one kid would want to beat up another. Now, she has moved beyond this, yet she recognizes that other kids, like Elizabeth, may still be stuck where she was. In other words, she is seeing the world as others see it, and not assuming that everyone thinks as she does.

If she was thinking at that level, she's combining three ICPS skills in her story: *sequenced planning, understanding others' feel-*

ings, and *understanding underlying motives* from another person's point of view.

This kind of very deliberate thinking in creating her plan to stop a bully, and in reflecting how bullying can affect others, can have an important impact on how Sarah will treat her classmates and others in the future.

In Real Life

Making Friends

Mark, age twelve, comes from an ICPS family. Thanks to his skills training, he was able to make a new friend by combining *listening* and *understanding motives*. Mark had been avoiding a boy at school who, on the surface, appeared to be very cheerful and strong, but also was very unfriendly and aloof. One day, Mark noticed that the boy looked sullen, a *nonverbal* cue, and asked what was wrong.

"Nothin'," the boy snapped.

As Mark started to walk away, the boy said, very quietly, "I can't believe my mom and dad are divorced. I'm so used to them both being around. Now Mom found someone she likes and I don't like him much."

Mark, a child of divorce himself, now had a new understanding of why the boy acted in such an unfriendly manner, and tried to comfort him. He told him to look at the bright side. "Maybe she'll end up not liking him or maybe he'll end up being nicer 'cause he's just trying to impress you now. Everything will turn out okay 'cause you'll get used to it."

Another boy, Christopher, told me that he also learned about a classmate by using his *listening skills* and *understanding motivation*. The classmate, Charles, told Chris that he recently found out that his mother had been married before, and had children who lived in another state. I asked Christopher if he felt any differently about Charles now, and Chris said, "I feel sorry for him because I know what's bothering him."

Mark felt *empathy* for his new friend, and Christopher felt *sympathy*. Neither boy had these feelings before they gained insight into their friends. They accomplished this by *listening* and coming to understand the *underlying motives* for their behavior. In other words, they remembered from earlier ICPS exercises that *things are not always what they seem to be*, and that there is *more than one possible reason* for why people do what they do. And these new insights brought both sets of boys closer together.

Nicholas also had an opportunity to apply a combination of three ICPS skills in the process of working out feelings about a classmate, John. Nicholas was interested in becoming John's friend, but John tended to pick fights. Though Nicholas knew that John felt bad inside because he was fat, he was still leery of becoming John's friend. His mom used ICPS dialoguing to talk with him about what he could do next:

Mom: How do you feel about him now that you know he feels bad inside?

Nicholas: I feel sorry for him, but that's no reason to bully people.

Mom: Do you think he needs a friend?

Nicholas: Mom, I still don't know what he's going to do.

Mom: What could you do or say to find out if he would still hurt people?

Nicholas: I could tell him I'll be his friend if he wants me to, but only if he stops hurting people.

Mom: And what might happen then?

Nicholas: He might say okay. But I'll wait a while to see how he acts.

Mom: And how long will that take?

Nicholas: A week. Then I'll know he means it.

Mom: Good thinking, Nicholas. You're thinking this through very well.

Nicholas's mom helped her son to think of *solutions* so Nicholas could figure out if he wanted to befriend John. Nicholas also considered the potential *consequences* of doing this. Because Nicholas understood the importance of time and timing, part of *sequenced planning*, he decided to wait and see how John would act, recognizing that it might well be too soon to become John's friend. This was part of his plan to gauge John's *motives*. It's significant to note that even though Nicholas had new insight into why John acted the way he did, Nicholas didn't change his relationship with John right away. Now that Nicholas could combine his ICPS skills, he was more likely to befriend John than Raymond, whom I described in Chapter 5. Nicholas had been able to focus on why Raymond might be a bully ("acting like his father"), but at that point chose to think no further about it.

Importantly, Nicholas also came to understand why another classmate, Zachary, had to keep bragging about how popular he was. It made him feel as if he had friends when he didn't. But Nicholas was able to recognize that it would be easier to befriend a boy like Zachary because, as he put it, "bragging doesn't physically hurt people."

Leaving Friendships Behind

Sometimes, children want to get out of a friendship and don't know how. Even parents can have a hard time in this situation. Unsure of what advice to give, they may try to dissuade their kids, by saying something like, "Try to be nice. Otherwise, you won't have any friends."

Dawn, age eight, found herself in this situation. Fortunately, her mother was versed in ICPS, and she handled the situation this way:

Mom: It's okay if you don't want to be Sherry's friend now. But before you really end it, think carefully about why you want to do that.

Dawn: I don't know. No one likes her. She's hanging around with mean kids.

Mom: Think about how you can tell her you don't want to be her friend.

Dawn: I don't want to hurt her feelings. But she keeps asking me to play.

Mom: What can you do or say?

Dawn: Just stay away from her and not say anything. Maybe she'll get the hint.

Mom: That's *one* way. How might that make her feel?

Dawn: Sad if she really still wants to be my friend.

Mom: And how would that make you feel inside?

Dawn: Sad.

Mom: Can you think of one good thing about her?

Dawn: She has a good singing voice.

Mom: How can you use that now?

Dawn: I can tell her I like her voice but not her friends.

Mom: Good thinking. You've given her the choice of who she wants to be friends with.

This dialogue took into account the *feelings* of both girls, and also helped Dawn think of *alternative solutions*.

When eight-year-old Beth was being mean to her friend Emily, her father used several ICPS skills to help his daughter think through her behavior.

Father: What's the problem? Why don't you want to say
hello to your friend?

Beth: She teases me. She thinks my hair is funny.

Father: Why do you think she thinks that?

Beth: 'Cause she thinks *her* hair is great.

Father: Is there any other possible reason she might tease
you? Think hard.

Beth: Maybe she really doesn't like her hair?

Father: That's one possibility. Can you think of another?

Beth: Maybe her father yelled at her today?

Father: Would you not say hello to her if you knew she
really didn't like her own hair, or if her father yelled at
her today?

Beth: She doesn't have to tease me.

Father: How do you think she feels when you don't talk
to her?

Beth: Sad.

Father: And how do you feel about her feeling sad?

Beth: Sad.

Father: Can you think of what to do so you both won't
feel sad and so she won't stop talking to you?

Beth: I can ask her why she's teasing me.

Father: And what else can you do?

Beth: Maybe if I invite her to my birthday party she won't
tease me.

By asking Beth to think about why Emily was teasing her,
Beth's dad was asking her to think about Emily's *underlying
motives*. When he asked Beth to think about how both she and
her friend felt, he let her know that he cares about how she
feels—and that he wants her to care too. By asking, "And how
do you feel about her feeling sad?" he was helping his daughter
develop *empathy*. And by asking her to think of what she could

do to get Beth to stop teasing her, he fostered the ICPS skill of *alternative solutions.*

This ICPS dialogue differs greatly from the Explaining Approach he had used in the past. Before ICPS, he would say things like, "If you aren't nice to people, how will they know you like them? You'd be very unhappy if she acted that way to you. If you keep acting that way, soon you won't have any friends. No one will even talk to you."

Most likely, Beth never heard a word of this. Fortunately for both of them, ICPS helped: as Beth's father became less concerned with social graces and more concerned with his daughter's feelings and the motives for her behavior, he was able to guide her to solve her problem on her own. In time, Beth became more empathic and more likely to think about what she was doing before coming to quick and possibly faulty conclusions about people.

Coping with Intimidation

Another common problem of friendships among the eight-through twelve-year-old set crops up when a group of kids gangs up on someone, often to scare or intimidate her. Twelve-year-old Francine, whom we met in Chapter 7, grew upset during a pajama party when a group of girls she considered her friends began to tell late-night horror stories they swore were true. When she became scared and told them she wanted to go home, they started telling her stories about what happens to people who are scared. After an hour, they finally stopped and went to sleep. The next morning, back at home, Francine told her mom, "I thought they were trying to destroy me."

Francine's mom's first thought was to tell her daughter to just stay away from those girls, but she used ICPS to help her think this through:

Mom: Are these girls your friends?

Francine: I thought they were.

Mom: How do you feel about them now?

Francine: I'm not sure. Maybe they were just fooling around.

Mom: Do you still want to be their friend?

Francine: I don't know.

Mom: What is it about them that attracts you to them?

Francine: They're usually very nice.

Mom: What can you say to them to let them know how you feel about what they did?

Francine: I can tell them I didn't like what they did. But I won't tell them I was scared or they'll think I'm a cry-baby.

This was a good plan. It gives Francine time to determine whether the girls are going to persist in scaring her, or if what happened at the pajama party was an isolated event.

When Parents Want a Friendship to End

Unfortunately, there are some kids who seem to exert a bad influence on other kids. Parents are often quick to let their kids know about these detrimental relationships. However, what they usually say is, "I don't want you hanging around those kids any more"—which only makes them more attractive. Using ICPS skills is much more effective.

If your child seems caught up in a destructive friendship, ask him or her:

- How do you feel when you're around those kids?
- What is it about them that you like?
- Do you like the way you feel around them?

- What can happen if you stay friends with those kids?
- Do you want that to happen?
- What can you do so that will not happen?

Many kids this age want to talk to parents about these issues. Posing questions like the ones above and encouraging follow-up conversation helps them not only deal with the problems they are facing now, but also prepares them to resist the peer pressure they'll experience as teenagers that could lead to more serious problems, as I will discuss in the Epilogue. If your child is befriending youngsters who seem likely to put your child at risk, now is the time to help him plan a course of action to avoid this eventuality.

In addition to developing the ability to choose, make, and keep friends, children need to develop two other skills if they wish to become successful, competent adults: the ability to cope with disappointment and the ability to wait for what they want.

When youngsters can't wait, or if they fly off the handle at the drop of a hat, it's either because they can't or don't think of what else they can do. As a result, they react either angrily or impulsively, take their feelings out on others, or give up too soon.

Two types of children are at risk for causing serious harm to themselves and others in later life: those who do whatever it takes to get what they want when they want it, even at the risk of hurting others emotionally or physically; and those who walk away in despair of never getting what they want. Although most children who experience disappointments and frustrations do not turn against themselves or others, all children can learn to cope with these stresses in ways that will give them more satisfaction in life—now and later.

Coping with Disappointment

Many of life's problems involve disappointment. We are all disappointed at one time or another, though some of us cope with it better than others. The same is true of kids. Perhaps your child didn't get the part he wanted in the school play, or didn't make the baseball team. By age eleven or twelve, some children feel disappointed when the boy or girl they like doesn't like them back, or they aren't invited to a school dance. They are also disappointed when they receive a lower grade than they think they deserve, or when they don't get the presents they want for the holidays or their birthday.

According to Sarah's mother, Sarah always felt disappointed on her birthday. When she received her presents, she always found something wrong with them. The year she turned ten, she stormed into her parents' room and said with scorn, "I wanted in-line skates *and* a CD player, and I only got the skates."

"She was very lippy," Sarah's mom told me. In the past, she used to respond by belittling her daughter by saying, "What's wrong with you! Why are you so ungrateful!" Even after she started to learn ICPS, Sarah's mother still had trouble using the approach. First she tried, "We got you great things, and you should appreciate them." When that didn't work, she tried making *suggestions*, such as "We're really sorry you feel that way. Why don't you save your money and buy the CD player yourself?"

This time, Sarah's parents changed statements into questions, using ICPS dialogues. They asked, "Can you think of a reason why we didn't buy both of the big presents you wanted?"

Sarah had to think very hard about this. She had never been asked that question before. Finally she offered, " 'Cause you didn't want me to have them?"

"That's one possibility," her mom responded. However, she had a different reason in mind. So she asked, "Why else?"

" 'Cause it's too expensive?" asked Sarah.

"Well," replied her dad, "we did get you the skates, and some little presents too. We thought you'd like them." Sarah now recognized that her parents were trying to please her, not disparage her. Her parents then added, "If you really want a CD player, what can you do to get it?"

"I can save my allowance," said Sarah.

Sarah's parents could see the difference in how Sarah responded when they used ICPS and when they did not. And Sarah not only saw her parent's *point of view*, but she was also able to think of *alternative solutions* to the problem.

Using ICPS skills in combination also helped Sarah cope with a different disappointment. When she didn't get the grade she thought she would on a test, she first blamed the teacher. Then she recognized that maybe she didn't study hard enough. This represented a big breakthrough. Sarah was able to zero in on a reason for her poor grade that was within her control. Because she had had practice scheduling her time so she could complete all her homework, she decided to make a similar plan for studying for the next test. First she figured out how much time she'd need to study. Then she decided to begin studying several days ahead of time, instead of waiting until the day before. Sarah's mother helped her determine how many minutes she'd need to devote to studying each day. In the past, she would have said things like, "If you studied harder, you would have done better." Now, she and Sarah worked on ICPS skills together, and Sarah welcomed her help instead of resisting it.

Children this age also tend to be disappointed when their wishes to be with their friends conflict with their parents' safety concerns. Nicholas, for example, wanted to go to the mall with some of his friends, but was not allowed to go without a chaperon. In the past, this argument ended in a stalemate, and with Nicholas feeling frustrated and thwarted.

But when his mom began learning ICPS, she broached the subject of their disagreement in a different way:

Mom: What can happen if you go to the mall without a chaperon?

Nicholas: Nothing!

Mom: Think hard. What *could* happen?

Nicholas: I guess it's not always safe. There could be some older kids walking around who would hassle us. But the other kids will think I'm a dork if you come with us.

Mom: How do you think I feel when you boys are at the mall by yourselves?

Nicholas: Worried, I guess.

Mom: Can you think of a way to solve this problem so I won't worry, and the kids won't think you're a dork?

Nicholas: Maybe you could chaperon, but don't let the guys see you?

Mom: That's an idea. How can we do that?

Nicholas: You could walk behind us. You can see us but we won't see you.

Nicholas's mom accepted this solution. Instead of commanding her son to comply, she helped him to consider both *her* feelings and the potential consequences of going to the mall unsupervised. ICPS also enabled Nicholas to come up with a solution that satisfied everyone—including his friends' parents, who agreed to rotate chaperon duty when the boys went to the mall on weekends.

Often children are acutely disappointed when a friend can't keep a play date, or a parent can't keep a promise. Thomas, age nine, was supposed to go to a basketball game with his dad. Thomas completed his homework before dinner, and was very excited about the game, but his dad phoned to say he had to work late. And Mom couldn't take him because she had to stay home with his younger brother. Before ICPS, his dad would have tried to explain to Thomas why he couldn't get home in time to make the game—a futile effort, for Thomas wouldn't be comforted. Saying things like, "I know you're disappointed," or suggesting that he spend the evening reading his new book wouldn't comfort him either.

But with ICPS under his belt, Dad tried a whole new approach. He called Thomas from his office and began a dialogue to help his son cope with this frustration:

Dad: How do you feel about not being able to go to the game tonight?
Thomas (drawing upon his new feeling words): Frustrated. And disappointed.
Dad: How do you think I feel that I can't take you?
Thomas: Disappointed too.
Dad: Can you think of something different to do tonight that will make you feel happy?
Thomas: NO!
Dad: I know you can think of something. You're a good problem solver now.
Thomas: I could go on-line with a friend.
Dad: Good thinking. And if your friend isn't home, what else can you do?
Thomas: I'll play a game on the computer.

Thomas's tone of voice had changed by this point in the conversation. He realized that he'd enjoy playing computer games. Because Thomas's father *asked* his son how he felt—instead of telling him how he should feel—and then asked Thomas to come up with an alternative evening activity, Thomas felt respected and was able to think of an idea that pleased him.

But after a pause, he let it be known that he still wanted his dad to take him to a game. "Can you take me to the game next weekend?" he asked.

Be careful before you answer a question like this. If you persist in making promises that you can't keep, this will create a new problem: you may lose your child's trust. Take your time, make plans for another day—and hope your boss doesn't have an emergency.

Donna faced disappointment too. Emerging from her shell, she decided that she wanted to play softball after school. But the other girls wouldn't let her join in. It wasn't that they didn't like her—they did. But Donna was not skilled enough to play to the girls' satisfaction. Before ICPS, Donna would have interpreted a setback like this in the worst possible light. She probably would have assumed that the girls didn't want to include her, and that athletics were not for her. Now she was able to think about whether she wanted to practice and get better, or try to learn something else. She chose to learn gymnastics. Not only did she come to love the activity, but she made new friends too. Soon, she forgot about softball completely.

But life is never disappointment-free. Donna was tremendously excited about performing in her first gymnastics exhibition, only to find out that her parents had other obligations that night and would not be able to attend. But thanks to ICPS, Donna could now cope with this too, by "not thinking about it" and "looking at the bright side." When I asked her what she meant by "the bright side," she said, "Some kids don't get to do this at all." Donna has learned to cope very well.

Whether the problem causes a momentary setback or something more permanent, avoid telling your child how he feels, or how to reach his goal. Try not to say things like, "In ten years you won't even remember this." He just might. Instead, help your child understand the *underlying motives* of others, think about what else she can do, and if the goal is long-range, develop a *plan*. If your child's goal is unrealistic, try to guide her to a different goal. Urging a child to try harder to achieve a pipe dream, or urging her on by saying, "I know you can do it," may cause her to stop trying altogether, or cause her to feel like a failure. As you can see, Donna found satisfaction in her new endeavor, and your child can too.

Coping with Having to Wait: In Fictitious Situations

Many children have trouble waiting for what they want, whether it's for an adult to help or pay attention to them, for the weekend to arrive, or for their birthday. Often, the same children who have trouble coping with disappointment have trouble when a desire cannot be gratified immediately.

You can start helping kids learn to wait by playing the "What Can You Do While You Wait" game. Introduce the exercise by saying:

Terry wanted his mother to help him practice his violin lesson, but his mom was busy reading a book to his younger sister. Now you tell me five things Terry could do while he waits.

Not all children will be able to think of five things, but parents can help them by encouraging them to think of *alternative* ways to solve this problem. Here's a list of waiting activities that one of our ten-year-old ICPS boys came up with:

- Terry can talk to a friend on the phone
- Listen to the story with his sister
- Do his homework or read a book

- Watch TV
- Practice by himself

Before this boy had practiced ICPS, he was able to think of only one waiting strategy, "Try to play it by himself." His second solution, "He should just wait," merely restated the problem and was not a solution at all. Using ICPS helped him generate many good answers to a question that had previously stymied him.

Donna said a girl who was forced to wait could write an ICPS story; another girl, who had trouble waiting, said, "She could take a nap."

Waiting in Real Life

When your child has to wait for something in her day-to-day life, help her learn to wait by combining the timing element of the *sequenced planning* skill with *alternative solutions*. You could ask, for example, "Is this a good time or not a good time to ask me to help you with your homework?" If your child replies that it's not a good time, ask her, "What can you do while you wait?"

Eleven-year-old Eron felt that she wasn't getting enough of her mom's attention. Unfortunately, Eron's mom often wasn't home from her job until 7:30 at night, which was a significant source of guilt for her. However, when she did return home, she felt as if she needed some time to herself and would try to read the newspaper. Eron, eager for her mother's attention, would try to talk to her. In the past, her mom would say, "I really want to talk to you, but I'm reading now. I had a long day at work, and I need some time to myself." At this point, Eron's impatience would often get the better of her, and she'd stomp up to her room.

But after ICPS, their dialogue changed. Now her mom would say, "I really want to talk to you, but is this a good time or not a good time for us to talk? Can you think of why I need some time to relax?"

"You're tired," Eron volunteered. "I'll think of something different to do while I wait."

This exercise was eye-opening for Eron's mother as well. She came to realize that her almost adolescent daughter really did want to talk to her and ask her advice—and this desire to connect may not last forever. With Eron's adolescence just a few years away, Eron's mother realized that her daughter's needs might soon change, and that she should talk to her daughter while her daughter was still willing. ICPS helped Eron appreciate her mother's needs, and her mother to appreciate Eron's needs as well.

Even though Sarah had come a long way, she still occasionally forgot her ICPS and reacted impatiently when she couldn't get what she wanted. Thinking of five things to do while she waits in a fictitious situation helped temper her impulses when she wanted something immediately in real life.

For Donna, this exercise had a different importance. Lacking assertiveness, Donna tended to wait too long for what she wanted. If one of her parents or a classmate said, "Later," Donna would wait, sometimes never to receive what she wanted. Thanks to this exercise, she learned to distinguish how long she could reasonably be asked to wait, to occupy herself during that time, and then to use her newly acquired skill of *alternative solutions* if she wanted to try asking for what she wanted again.

With their increased ability to think of what to do while they waited, Sarah learned more patience, and Donna learned the difference between patient waiting and neglect. With these new skills, children can not only learn to wait when they can have what they want, but to cope with the frustration when they cannot.

As I mentioned earlier, ICPS dialoguing may seem at first to take too long, or feel too cumbersome. However, after you and your child are comfortable with the approach, you can shorten the dialogues. In the next chapter, I will show you how.

Summing Up

- When possible, help your child use more than one ICPS skill at a time. Start with just two skills. Add "how people feel" to "alternative solutions," for example, and then add another, such as "what might happen next?" Soon your child will be able to create a plan of action based on his understanding of how people feel and why they do what they do.

"What's in It for Me?"
and Other Questions Parents
Ask about ICPS

*Parents who think more about what their children do
also think more about what they themselves do.*

Now that you and your child are familiar with the full array of ICPS skills, you may still have some questions about using this approach in your day-to-day life with your child.

"Can ICPS dialogues be shortened?"

The most frequent question I hear from parents who are novices at this method is, "These dialogues are too long! Can't we make them shorter?"

Fortunately, the answer is yes, though perhaps not at first. In the beginning, it's best to move in a deliberate and methodical way, so that both you and your child learn the method. But in time—and how much time depends on each family—the dialogues can certainly be shortened. After you and your child are comfortable with ICPS, you may only need one sentence or phrase to help your child think about a problem at hand and how to solve it.

Depending upon the nature of the problem, you can decide whether you want to ask him about his or someone else's *feel-*

ings, about thinking of a *solution* to the problem, thinking of a *consequence* of the solution, or about creating a *plan* of action. For example, if your son is yelling at his sister, you can ask him, "Can you think of a different way to tell your sister how you feel?" Because your son can now anticipate the next questions— "How do you think your sister feels when you yell at her?" "What might happen if you yell at her like that?"—you may no longer have to ask them.

If you want him to focus on his sister's feelings, you may also find that your question, "How do you think your sister feels when you yell at her like that?" is sufficient. If you choose this question, remember to ask, not tell. At first some parents find themselves reverting back to the Explaining Approach, as in, "Your sister feels angry when you yell at her."

The question, "What can you do to solve this problem?" (asking for a solution) or, "What can you do first?" (asking for a plan) may suffice when, for example, your child wants to regain the trust of a recently betrayed friend. If your child has just told a lie, taken something without permission, or hurt another emotionally or physically, you can ask, "What might happen when . . . ?" If your child still isn't showing empathy, you can ask, "What else might happen?" as a follow-up question. And if your child is still focusing on what might happen to *him,* not the other person, continue with two additional questions: "How might that make your friend feel?" and "How will you feel about that?"

Other examples of how only one or two questions can replace the full ICPS dialogues can be found in Chapter 11, where I have created a quiz to help you identify different parenting styles.

"If I let my child think for himself, won't I lose control?"

Many parents who haven't yet tried ICPS worry that the method will put them at a disadvantage—that they won't be in control of their children or of life around the house. But I ask you to consider if you are in control now. If your child is bullying or teasing others, or refusing to clean her room or come up with a plan for completing her homework, chances are you already feel out of control.

My point is that by using ICPS, and giving your child a sense of control, you will gain control back. Your child will behave in ways that have fewer negative consequences, and you won't find yourself constantly being engaged in power plays.

A man who called in to a radio program while I was being interviewed told us how he had appreciated being given the freedom to think when he was a child. "When I was about eight, I smacked my little brother for stepping on my robot," he said. "My father talked to me for about a half hour about it." I asked the caller how he felt about the fact that his father chose to talk to him instead of spanking him. He said he felt empowered: "It was my decision to apologize. I felt very bad inside, and I never did that again." He added that had his father spanked him, or demanded that he apologize, he never would have had the opportunity to experience the bad feelings he did, and that being allowed to have these feelings is what prevented him from hurting others for the rest of his life.

Although we don't know exactly *how* this man's father talked to him at the time, it was very important to him that his father let him decide what to do.

"If I use ICPS, will my child think he can do anything he wants?"

Giving your child control does not mean he has freedom to do as he pleases. It means empowering your child, and giving him the confidence that comes with knowing he can make good decisions. I have described children who decide *how* to clean their rooms, not *whether* to clean them, and *how* to be responsible for other household chores, not *whether* to do them. You have also seen how children can learn to make good decisions—such as coming home at the expected time after school—by learning to appreciate your feelings about this.

Suppose your son is getting angrier and angrier at his sister because she won't give him the magazine she's reading. You can shorten the dialogue by asking him, "Can you think of a different way to tell your sister what you want?"

He might say, "Yeah, I can knock her out."

In this case, continue the dialogue by asking, "And what might happen if you do that?" If your child continues to give solutions that will have negative consequences, your child is not yet ready for the shortened dialogues. By continuing the dialogue, you are not letting him do whatever he wants. Rather, you are helping him think of solutions that will not hurt his sister, his friends, you—or ultimately, himself.

"Is it always appropriate to use ICPS?"

Parents also ask me if there are times when using ICPS is *not* appropriate. In fact, there are times when I don't recommend that parents use the problem-solving approach. Suppose your child darts out into the street in the face of an oncoming car. You'd hardly stop to ask, "Is that a good place to be?" or "Is running in the street a good idea?" First, you'd pull your child to safety, and then you'd both need some time to collect yourselves.

You may well be tempted to yell at your child, or to explain why what she did was so dangerous, but I suggest you refrain. Neither yelling at her nor explaining will prevent her from dashing out in the street again. Only using ICPS will help ensure that she's more careful in the future. But ICPS doesn't work when people are stressed or emotionally upset. Wait until you have both calmed down—but don't wait too long, or the problem will be long forgotten. Then begin an ICPS dialogue. Ask her to tell you what she should do before crossing the street (she knows by now to look both ways), what might happen if she does not, how she (and you) will feel if that happens, and what she can do so that will not happen.

"My child has ADHD. Can ICPS help?"

Bonnie Aberson, who has used ICPS with many teachers and families for almost fifteen years, recently taught ICPS to parents of three eight-year-olds with Attention Deficit Hyperactivity Disorder (ADHD), two boys and one girl. All three youngsters became dramatically less depressed and had fewer discipline problems when observed six months later. These children also learned how to plan tasks and carry them out, how to express their feelings, and how to get along better with others. And, importantly, their mothers mentioned that they found themselves listening to their children more than they did before.

One of the boys, initially very dependent on his mother, had trouble getting ready for school on time. One day, during the program, this boy asked his mother for an allowance. His mother asked him what he could do to get an allowance, and the boy answered, "I can pick up the leaves around the pool and water the plants." The next day he woke up his parents, got dressed, and was ready for school. When his mom asked (very surprised), "Why are you up so early?" he said, "I want to get my job done before I go to school so I can play with my friend after school." This anecdote shows that, together with help in planning activities such as laying out his clothes the night before, this boy was able to think ahead in ways he never did before.

Aberson reports that three years later, the parents have continued to use the ICPS dialoguing techniques successfully with their children. The girl, who initially had few friends, did poorly in school, and had little interest in other activities, now gets good grades, does her homework independently, has learned to play the piano, and is active in the Girl Scouts. Also three years later, the boys are functioning more independently at home and at school and have more friends than ever before.

"What's in it for me?"

Once parents come to understand how ICPS can help their children, I always sense that many also want to know, "What's in it for me?" I have been able to help parents see that by helping their children learn to think about what *they* do, parents often begin to think about themselves, and how they act with coworkers, friends, spouses, and children.

One mother, Carolyn Wallace, told me that since she started using ICPS at home she not only thinks more now about how she talks to her children, but how she talks to her coworker. In the past, the two women would quarrel and Carolyn would say things like, "How do you expect me to do your work and my work!" As a result, the women became more and more estranged. But after learning ICPS, she turned to her coworker and said, "You know, we've got a problem and I need your help to solve it." Both women were surprised at the change. Sure enough, they began to talk to each other, and today they not only work well together but are good friends outside of work.

Just as we help children learn to express their feelings when they feel hurt inside, we can learn the lesson ourselves. Doreen Block, a woman who often felt very shy among other adults, was waiting for her son's school bus to arrive with her friend Gloria and another woman Gloria knew. Right in front of Doreen, Gloria invited the other woman to a party she was having. Because Doreen was using ICPS at home, she said, "I feel sad that I'm not invited to your party." Gloria felt awful. It was a mere oversight on her part, but an oversight that might not have been addressed if Doreen hadn't felt safe enough to assert her feelings.

Another benefit of using the ICPS method is that some parents come to think more about how their own actions may contribute to their child's behavior. Eight-year-old Benji, for example, was an extremely dependent child. His parents were growing increasingly exasperated with him because, as his mom put it, "He wanted us to pour his cereal, put his tape in the VCR, even sharpen his pencil. He wouldn't do his homework himself. He'd say he didn't understand it before he even read it." Not knowing what to do, his parents vacillated between saying, "Do it yourself," and just doing it for him.

While Benji's parents recognized that before ICPS they had done too much for him when he was a toddler, they didn't know what to do to change their son's behavior. Now they were able to use the skills of ICPS to help their son overcome his incessant dependence.

They asked Benji to list five things he wanted his mom and dad to do for him. Assuring him that they'd be there to help him, they asked him to choose just one to try himself. Benji decided he'd try to pour his own cereal. Using *sequenced steps*, Benji's mom asked him to get the cereal and put it on the table, and then get the milk. "But what if I spill it?" he asked, laughing. He'd recognized an obstacle from his ICPS games. His parents, also smiling, watched him pour the cereal, and then, with great deliberation, pour the milk as well. No spills, and smiles all around.

They decided that was enough independence for one day. But the next day, when Benji asked, "Please put this tape in the VCR for me," he laughed at his own request and then said, "I can do that."

Getting Benji to do his homework independently took a little longer. Benji's dad wanted his son to approach his homework with joy instead of trepidation. Math was a subject Benji particularly disliked. Adapting a game from *I Can Problem Solve*, the workbook for the intermediate elementary grades, Benji's dad used numbers to play the popular party game called "Memory," or, as some call it, "Concentration." Rather than matching pictures, however, this game is played by matching, for example, a number (25) with its multiples (5 x 5). Although Benji's father suggested the game, Benji soon joined in by creating his own cards that would allow him to test his subtraction and addition skills. Benji enjoyed this game so much he adapted it for other subjects. For science, for instance, he made cards matching an animal with its means of locomotion, such as fish/swim, horse/gallop, bird/fly.

Now that Benji was in the mood to learn, Benji's father decided it was time to tackle homework assignments. He began by asking Benji to read his homework assignments aloud to him, and to explain the instructions one at a time. This way, Benji learned to plan *sequenced steps* to complete a task. Soon, he became more self-confident and was able to deal with his homework assignments on his own.

Just as Benji's parents recognized the role they played in their son's dependence before ICPS, eight-year-old Billy's mom gained insight, while using ICPS, about how she might have contributed to Billy's need to be a perfectionist. She told me, "If he made even simple mistakes on his homework, or answered a question incorrectly in school, he would get very upset, often blaming others for his mistakes. His art teacher, who said he did lovely work in art, also said he was so slow that when other children finished their projects, he was still just starting." And Billy's response to that problem was, "Well, I don't care because the other kids just rush and don't care how their work looks and I want mine to be good."

Billy's mom used to try to change his need to be so perfect by saying things like, "You just drew a great house. I bet it's the best in your class." But that only made Billy feel more anxious because he felt it could be better. If he got a bad grade in school, she would say, "That's okay, but I know you can do better." In gym, he would stop himself from learning how to use the gymnastics equipment saying, "I can't do it." And his mom would say, "Yes, you can do it."

As she taught her son to think about others' *underlying motives* for why they do what they do, she began to think about *why* she was pressuring her son, however unintentionally. Her parents had told her she was "special" ever since she was five years old. "That put a very heavy responsibility on me. I didn't know what I was good at. I felt different from my classmates. I felt I had to rise above them. I felt isolated from them socially," she explained.

Once Billy's mother realized her role in Billy's problem, she was able to help him change. One day, when he drew a house, she initiated an ICPS dialogue:

> *Mom*: How do you feel about what you've just drawn?
> *Billy*: Frustrated. I can make it better.
> *Mom*: Tell me about your drawing.
> *Billy*: This is our house. But it doesn't look like our house.
> *Mom*: Does it really have to? Tell me *one* thing you like about this picture.
> *Billy*: The window.

Billy started to laugh and drew designs on the window. Mom laughed too. Billy started drawing designs, some very silly ones, on the roof and then on the door. He got so carried away that he forgot he didn't like the house. Finally, he was free to be creative. No longer did he feel the need to be "perfect."

Next, Billy's mom could help him change his unrealistic expectations about his school performance. Rather than *explaining* why he didn't need to get all A's on his report card, she used ICPS to help him create more realistic goals that he could reach, and that he could feel good about.

One of our ICPS fathers revealed that he too had been overly praised as a child. But he took another direction than Billy's mom; instead of trying to live up to unrealistic expectations, he stopped trying to succeed in school and, for a while, stopped trying to make friends. "I needed to show them I wasn't so special after all," he told me, his eyes full of scorn. As a result of this upbringing, when he became a father, he hardly praised his daughter at all. And she eventually stopped trying to succeed as well, for exactly the opposite reason. ICPS helped this dad understand how his own lack of sensitivity to his daughter's feelings made her unconcerned about her own sense of pride.

As you can see, ICPS helps some parents gain insight into how their own pasts may have affected their child's behavior. Other parents learn to see how they were contributing to their child's problem in the present. One mom came to understand how she may have created a need for her daughter, Victoria, age twelve, to be deceptive. Before ICPS, this mom primarily used the Power Approach. Here's an example: One day, she told Victoria to come right home after school to study math since she was failing that subject. Instead, Victoria went to her Girl Scouts meeting, assuming that her mom, who was at work, wouldn't find out. But her mom did find out—from a neighbor. When questioned about her whereabouts, Victoria lied, infuriating her mother even more. She then demanded that Victoria return her merit badges.

In time, she came to see what a devastating blow this was to Victoria. Once she switched to the ICPS method, she stopped demanding that Victoria return home after school to study, and instead asked Victoria to make a *sequenced plan* that would allow her daughter to study and also attend her beloved Girl Scouts meetings. With a calendar in hand, Victoria scheduled in hours for schoolwork and for Scouts. And instead of feeling angry, frustrated, and resentful, Victoria felt proud of her planning abilities.

Sarah's mother came to realize that she was often too quick to punish her daughter without finding out her view of the problem. As Sarah once told me, "Mom never lets me tell her why I hit my little brother. She just gets mad and grounds me. But sometimes my brother does things that get me so mad, like going through my things and taking them." After learning ICPS, however, Sarah's mom began to see that sometimes hitting may be her daughter's solution, not the problem. Very proudly, she told me, "Now that I can dialogue with Sarah, she finds another way to let her brother know how she feels."

ICPS helped Joshua's dad to not only help his son but to understand himself. Joshua, age ten, had begged his father to let him take piano lessons. For the first two months, he practiced willingly and often. But then his interest waned. Joshua's dad recognized that by using the Power Approach to try to coerce Josh into practicing—by saying things like, "When are you going to stay with something you start! You said you wanted piano lessons and now look what's happening!"—he never allowed himself to hear his son's point of view.

And Joshua, who hated these harangues, was afraid to tell his father that he had lost interest in the piano. He just moped around the house, accepting that he couldn't play with his friends until he practiced his piano. Finally, his father realized that maybe he should ask Josh what was bothering him rather than simply yelling at him. Josh said, meekly, "I hate practicing piano. I'd rather play soccer."

Still not listening to his son, Dad yelled, "I don't want to waste my time and money for your soccer if you're not going to stay with it!" This made Josh feel even worse. And they were at a stalemate—until his dad began using ICPS. By using the problem-solving dialogues, father and son began to communicate in a way they never had before:

> *Dad*: It hurts me to work so hard to make money for this family, and have you waste it.
> *Josh*: Dad, I thought I'd like piano, but I can't be with my friends when I practice. And right now, I really want to be with my friends.

Dad: You really want to be with your friends?
Josh: Yes, I really like soccer and I can play soccer and be
   with my friends.

Josh's father began to understand that he had to consider his
son's perspective rather than simply focus on his own needs.

There's one more important example of how ICPS helped
one of our dads—Nicholas's father. Because he began using
ICPS to talk to his son about people's feelings, Nicholas's father
began to think about his own feelings as well. He discovered that
when Nicholas forgot to rake the leaves, an example I described
earlier, he not only felt angry but also hurt and disappointed in
his son, and unable to trust him. By realizing his own feelings,
and then helping Nicholas to appreciate them, Nicholas's father
was able to pay attention to his son's feelings—something he
hadn't been able to do before. As he described it to me, "When I
realized what was going on inside of me, I began talking to my
son in a different way." Then his expression and tone of voice
grew softer; he was visibly moved as he added, "Our relationship
changed."

In her book *KidStress*, Georgia Witkin tells us that about
15 percent of nine- through twelve-year-olds surveyed reported
that they were afraid of talking to their parents about things that
upset them for fear of making their parents angry. They also worried about being yelled at, or hurt. Now that you are familiar with
ICPS—and understand the importance of genuine listening,
appreciating each other's point of view, and two-way communica-
tion—your child will not be among that 15 percent.

None of the significant changes in the families I've described
happened overnight. Both kids and parents had to invest time to
learn the method, especially in Sarah's and Donna's families. Yet
they accepted the time commitment because they recognized
that the approaches they were using in the past weren't working.
Even though the Problem-Solving Approach may take longer,

most parents with whom I have worked have assured me that this new approach is well worth the effort. One parent told me, "At first it was very difficult to remember to ask, not tell. I really had to think about what I was doing. It's second nature to me now. I don't know how I talked any other way."

And comments by their children heightened their enthusiasm. When I asked Nicholas if he liked ICPS, and why he thinks we wanted him to learn it, Nicholas said, "When I have a problem, I'll be prepared for it."

Sarah said, "I like school now, and I have friends."

Donna, looking very proud, smiled and told me, "I can solve problems now."

One sixth-grader probably put it best when she told me, "We have to learn to think for ourselves. People won't always be around to help us."

If you are using ICPS now, you are sending a powerful message that you trust your children to make good decisions. You can feel comfortable with that because you have given them the skills they will need to make those decisions. And your trust will be returned. One of our ICPS kids, age ten, told me, "I'm not afraid anymore to tell my parents when I do something wrong because I trust them not to hurt me."

When I heard that, I was electrified.

Summing Up

- As you talk with your child using ICPS, ask yourself, "Did I tell him or did I ask him how he feels?" "Did I tell him or did I ask him what to do next, and what might happen next if he does that?"

- You can eventually shorten ICPS dialogues with single questions or phrases, such as, "Can you think of a different way to tell me/him/her how you feel?" "What can you do (or do first) to solve this problem?" and "What might (did) happen when . . . ?"

- Avoid ICPS dialoguing in the heat of emotion. Your child will probably not be listening. Wait until your child calms down. You may want to calm down too.

- Helping children learn to think about what they do can help you think more about what you do—with coworkers, friends, your spouse, and your children.

- Any approach that intentionally or unintentionally hurts a child emotionally or physically will create a need in that child to attempt to regain control by hurting others, or perhaps to shut down and not respond at all.

◀ **11** ▶

An ICPS Quiz

When parents turn statements into questions, kids turn problems into problems to be solved.

Now that we've identified all the ICPS skills, alone and in combination, let's see how much you remember. I've composed a quiz to see how well you can distinguish the ICPS way of handling problems from the Power, Suggesting, and Explaining Approaches.

Below are examples of typical problems eight- to twelve-year-olds face. Each situation is followed by one or more responses representative of the four parenting styles described in this book. See if you can identify them. After you have identified the ICPS example, you can use it as a shortened version of the full-scale ICPS dialogues you have learned up to now. Answers follow each problem situation.

Problems between Children
and Their Siblings

Jealousy. An eight-year-old girl is jealous of her twin brother because, as she says, "He gets more sleep-overs than me." You respond by saying,

1. You have friends who invite you to sleep over.
2. Don't be jealous. You have things your brother doesn't.
3. What do you have that makes you feel really happy?
4. When are you going to stop complaining about your brother!

Answers: (1) explaining, (2) explaining, (3) problem solving (ICPS), (4) power (a put-down)

Annoyance. Eight-year-old Tom is bothered because his six-year-old sister Betsy is bugging him again. He screams at her to "Get out!"

You turn to Betsy and say,

1. This is not the time to bother your brother. He's doing his homework.
2. If you don't leave your brother alone, you'll have to go to your room.
3. Why don't you do your homework now?*
4. Is this a good time to talk to your brother?

*Even though this response begins with the word "why," it is not a genuine information-seeking question. There is no room for her to come up with an idea of her own.

Answers: (1) explaining, (2) power, (3) suggesting, (4) problem solving (ICPS)

To Tom, you say,

1. Don't yell at your sister like that. It's not nice.
2. Can you think of a different way to tell your sister how you feel?
3. I will not allow you talk to your sister like that!

Answers: (1) explaining, (2) problem solving (ICPS), (3) power

"It's his fault." An eight-year-old girl blames her older brother for everything, including a bad roll of the dice in a board game. "He made me toss bad," she whines. "His pieces are always in the way." You say to her,

1. It wasn't your brother's fault. We all have bad tosses sometimes.
2. Your brother won't play with you if you act like that.
3. Stop acting like a baby! He's not trying to hurt you.
4. What can you say to your brother if you think his pieces are in the way?
5. What might happen if you keep blaming your brother for everything?

Answers: (1) explaining, (2) explaining, (3) power (belittling) and explaining, (4) problem solving (ICPS), (5) problem solving (ICPS)

Fighting over the TV. Nine-year-old Keith and his eleven-year-old sister Lindsay want to watch different programs at the same time, and he changes the channel. You say to Keith,

1. What can you say or do when you both want to watch a different show at the same time?
2. Turn the channel back right now!

3. You're not being fair to your sister. She lets you watch shows you want.
4. What gives you the right to turn the channel?

Answers: (1) problem solving (ICPS), (2) power, (3) explaining, (4) power (the question isn't genuine, but accusatory)

Sharing a bedroom. Both nine-year-old Edward and seven-year-old Lewis want the top bunk bed. You say to both of them,

1. What can you two do to solve this problem?
2. Stop your bickering! If you can't decide, I'll decide who sleeps in the top bed.
3. You should take turns. That's the fair thing to do.

Answers: (1) problem solving (ICPS), (2) power, (3) suggesting and explaining

Borrowing without permission. A twelve-year-old girl is annoyed because her brother keeps using her computer when she needs it. You say to your son,

1. Your sister needs her computer now to do her homework.
2. How many times have I told you not to use your sister's computer!
3. How do you think your sister feels when you use her computer when she needs it?
4. Ask your sister when you want to use her things.
5. What might happen if you use her computer when she's doing her homework?

Answers: (1) explaining, (2) power, (3) problem solving (ICPS), (4) suggesting, (5) problem solving (ICPS)

Between Friends or Classmates

Thoughtlessness. Your eleven-year-old son asks if he can call his friend at 9:00 Sunday morning even though you've told him not to. You say,

1. Your friend is probably still sleeping. Call him later.
2. Your friend will be angry if you wake him up.
3. How do you think your friend will feel if you wake him up?
4. You're being very thoughtless. I told you not to call him now!
5. Is this a good time or not a good time to call him?

Answers: (1) explaining and suggesting, (2) explaining, (3) problem solving (ICPS), (4) power, (5) problem solving (ICPS)

Your twelve-year-old son decides to go to the high school to see what hours the pool is open though his friend is supposed to come over to play video games in five minutes. You say,

1. How will your friend feel if you're not here when he comes?
2. Your friend will feel very angry if you're not here.
3. If you act like this, you won't have any friends.
4. Leaving right before your friend comes is not very nice.
5. Is this a good time or not a good time to leave the house?

Answers: (1) problem solving (ICPS), (2) explaining, (3) explaining, (4) explaining, (5) problem solving (ICPS)

Your twelve-year-old daughter doesn't return things, such as a book her classmate needed to do her assignment. You say,

1. No one will let you borrow things if you don't give them back on time.

2. What might happen if you don't return her book now?*
3. The girl will feel very angry with you.
4. How do you think she will feel if you hold on to her book?

*If your child answers "She won't be my friend," or "She won't like me," ask, "What else might happen?" The goal is for your child to become sensitive to the impact of her act on others, not just what happens to her. If needed, you can guide her by asking, "What might happen if she doesn't get her homework done on time?"

Answers: (1) explaining, (2) problem solving (ICPS), (3) explaining, (4) problem solving (ICPS)

Broken trust. Your ten-year-old daughter is hurt because her friend revealed her secret to another girl. You say,

1. Tell her you're very hurt that she broke your trust.
2. If you're afraid to tell her you feel hurt, get a friend to tell her.
3. If you don't tell her how you feel, she'll keep on doing things like that.
4. What can you do or say when someone does that to you?

Answers: (1) suggesting, (2) suggesting, (3) explaining, (4) problem solving (ICPS)

Broken friendship. Your nine-year-old daughter whines, "My best friend likes the new kid more." You say,

1. Tell her you feel bad, and you still want to be her friend.
2. That's making you very sad, isn't it?
3. How does that make you feel?

4. Be friends with the new kid too.

5. What can you do or say so she'll still be your friend?

Answers: (1) suggesting, (2) explaining, (3) problem solving (ICPS), (4) suggesting, (5) problem solving (ICPS)

Taking things without asking. Your eight-year-old daughter complains, "She took my lunch box." You say,

1. Tell her if she doesn't give it back, you won't be her friend anymore.
2. Tell the teacher.
3. What can you do or say so she'll give it back?
4. Don't play with her anymore. She's not a nice person.

Answers: (1) suggesting, (2) suggesting, (3) problem solving (ICPS), (4) suggesting and explaining

Being teased. Your nine-year-old daughter whines, "She's calling me names." You say,

1. You've got to learn to ignore it.*
2. Tell the teacher.*
3. Tease her back. Don't just take that.*
4. What can you do or say so she'll stop teasing you?
5. Ask her why she does that.

*These suggestions offer different advice, but the same approach. The parent is doing the thinking for the child.

Answers: (1) suggesting, (2) suggesting, (3) suggesting, (4) problem solving (ICPS), (5) suggesting

Unjustified blame. Your twelve-year-old son comes home complaining that he got blamed at school for something he didn't do. You say,

1. Tell whoever did it to own up. It's not fair for you to take the blame.
2. Tell your teacher what happened.
3. Ask the person responsible why he's letting you take the blame, and then tell him how you feel. If you don't, he'll think he can get away with it next time.
4. I see you're very upset by this.
5. How can you let the person responsible know how you feel?

Answers: (1) suggesting and explaining, (2) suggesting, (3) suggesting and explaining, (4) explaining, (5) problem solving (ICPS)

Whistle-blowing. Your eight-year-old daughter is getting the reputation of being a tattler. You say,

1. If you keep tattling on others, you won't have any friends.
2. If you tattle on others, they'll tattle on you.
3. How might someone feel if you tattle on her?
4. What might happen if you keep tattling on someone?

Answers: (1) explaining, (2) explaining, (3) problem solving (ICPS), (4) problem solving (ICPS)

Between Parent and Child

Irresponsibility. Your eleven-year-old daughter forgets to relay phone messages. You say,

1. When are you going to remember to tell us who called!
2. People will think I'm not interested in talking to them.
3. People will think you're irresponsible.
4. What can you do to remember to give me my messages?

Answers: (1) power, (2) explaining, (3) explaining, (4) problem solving (ICPS)

Your ten-year-old son leaves his bike outside in the rain. You say,

1. What might happen if you leave your bike outside in the rain?
2. Your bike will get rusty if it gets wet.
3. Can't you ever do anything around here!
4. You'll be very upset if your bike gets ruined.

Answers: (1) problem solving (ICPS), (2) explaining, (3) power, (4) explaining

Lying. Your eleven-year-old son insists he didn't break the window—another boy threw the ball. You say,

1. I feel very angry that you're lying about this.
2. How do you think I feel when you don't tell the truth?
3. It's bad enough that you didn't listen to us about throwing against the house. Now you're lying about it too.
4. You'll pay for this out of your allowance.
5. Brad wasn't here that day. You're lying again.

Answers: (1) explaining, (2) problem solving (ICPS), (3) power, (4) power, (5) power

Thoughtlessness. Your eight-year-old daughter wakes you and your husband up on Saturday morning by coming into your bedroom when the door is closed. You say,

1. When are you going to learn to stay out of our room when the door is closed!
2. Stay out of our room when the door is closed unless it's really important.

3. If you don't stay out of our room, we'll have to put a lock on the door.
4. Why don't you play with your doll furniture until we wake up?
5. What can you do while you wait for us to wake up?

Answers: (1) power, (2) suggesting, (3) power, (4) suggesting, (5) problem solving (ICPS)

Back-talk. Your nine-year-old son says, "That's stupid," to his father. He says,

1. Don't back-talk me! I'm the father, you're the child. Do you understand this!
2. I feel very angry when you talk back to me.
3. Can you think of a different way to tell me how you feel?
4. Did you hear what you just said? You must learn how to talk to people or they won't want to talk to you.

Answers: (1) power, (2) explaining, (3) problem solving (ICPS), (4) explaining

You tell your eight-year-old daughter that she can't play with her friend that afternoon until she finishes her homework. She says, "Mommy, I HATE you." You say,

1. I don't hate you.
2. I know you're angry, but you have to do your homework.
3. How do you think I feel when you talk to me like that?
4. Can you think of a different way to tell me how you feel?

Answers: (1) explaining, (2) explaining, (3) problem solving (ICPS), (4) problem solving (ICPS)

Your nine-year-old son thinks he gets punished more than his sister, and says, "You love her more." You say,

1. No, it's not true. I love you both the same.
2. You know better than to think that!
3. Why do you think that?

Answers: (1) explaining, (2) power (put-down), (3) problem solving (ICPS)

One last question. Some parents are able to initiate an ICPS dialogue with their children, but are unable to finish it. Rather than remain with the Problem-Solving Approach, for example, they switch to either the Explaining or Suggesting Approach. Here's a talk between a dad and his eleven-year-old son Jeremy over an incident that happened at school. Dad began using the Problem-Solving Approach. Read the dialogue and see if you can find when he abandoned this approach, and which approach he began to use instead.

> *Jeremy*: Henry and I were wrestling and he hit me too hard, on purpose.
> 1 *Dad*: How did you feel when that happened?
> *Jeremy*: Mad.
> 2 *Dad*: What did you do about that?
> *Jeremy*: I told the teacher.
> 3 *Dad*: No, don't do that. Henry will get mad and you'll lose a friend. Just tell him you won't wrestle with him anymore if he doesn't play fair.

If you noticed that Jeremy's dad stopped using the ICPS method during comment #3, you're right. You're also correct if you recognize that he began using the Suggesting and Explaining Approaches instead.

How could Jeremy's dad have finished the dialogue with the Problem-Solving Approach?

When you and your child are completely comfortable with the Problem-Solving Approach, you can shorten the dialogues still more by simply saying, "Let's ICPS this." You may soon hear your child chanting this too.

Remember, ICPS is a *process*; it's not about content. By turning statements into questions, you are helping your child learn *how* to think, not what to think. This will help her turn her problems into problems to be solved.

If you have answered at least fifteen of the twenty-two questions in this quiz correctly, you are now an

OFFICIAL ICPS FAMILY

Congratulations!

Epilogue
Preventing Serious Problems in the Teen Years: Drug Abuse, Teen Pregnancy, Violence

Children who can solve problems important to them now will be able to solve problems important to them later.

This book has focused on everyday problems that come up in typical families. We've seen how the ICPS approach helps already well-adjusted and competent problem solvers like Nicholas become even more interpersonally skilled. It also helps aggressive youngsters like Sarah become more empathic, in control of their anger, and better problem solvers so that they can get along well with others. And it helps Donna and children like her become more assertive, better able to express their thoughts and feelings, and more skilled as they navigate their interpersonal worlds.

Though both Sarah and Donna had emotional and social difficulties, they will be able to find their way as they grow into teenagers and adults. But some children, especially those who are more extremely aggressive and socially withdrawn, will not, without help, be so lucky. Some youngsters will drop out of school too soon, become pregnant, begin abusing substances, and find themselves on a downward spiral.

In this Epilogue, I will show you how the Problem-Solving Approach can short-circuit the onset of the more serious problems on the rise among our nation's youth—substance abuse, teen pregnancy, and violence.

But before talking about ICPS in this context, I want to call your attention to some of the possible warning signs that suggest your child may be at risk for encountering serious problems as a teenager. We've already discussed some of these signs: changes in nonverbal cues, such as facial expression, tone of voice, and body posture; and chronic antisocial or withdrawn behavior, including an inability to make friends.

Other important signs include:

- An inability or unwillingness to express thoughts and feelings
- Childhood depression
- A drop in grades at school
- Estrangement from family, school, and community
- Becoming a victim of violence
- Having uncontrolled anger
- Associating with other peers at risk for serious problems
- Torturing or killing animals
- Inappropriate access to or possession of firearms

As discussed by the U.S. Office of Education in its publication *Early Warning, Timely Response: A Guide to Safe Schools* and sent to schools nationwide, if a child has any one of these risk factors, it doesn't mean with certainty that he will encounter serious problems in the years to come. Most children who do become drug abusers, pregnant, and/or violent during the teen years usually display more than one early warning sign.

However, research does indicate that these problems don't go away by themselves. Even preschoolers who engage in intense or frequent high-risk behaviors may need additional professional help and emotional support from family, friends, and community groups such as churches or synagogues. Understanding how

ICPS can add to the benefits of professional help and emotional supports can play a key role in helping your child prepare for the teen years and grow into a healthy, competent, and successful adult.

Drugs, Cigarettes, and Alcohol

"Just say no."

"Just don't do it."

These slogans are all too familiar. They make the problem sound simple—but as we all know, there's nothing simple about substance abuse.

Slogans are perfect examples of the Suggesting Approach—they tell youngsters what to do and what not to do. We've already seen how ineffective this approach can be. First, suggestions often fall on deaf ears. In addition, slogans don't stimulate youngsters to think for themselves about why they should or shouldn't use drugs, nor do they encourage kids to think of what they can do instead.

Finally, simplistic slogans ignore the reality of peer pressure. Why do some teens and preteens feel the need to succumb to it? They may simply not like themselves. Perhaps they have not been successful in making the friends they wanted, and, feeling lonely and frustrated, turn to a group of peers whom they perceive might become their friends. But the only way to insure acceptance by these new kids is to follow what they dictate.

Having these perceived "friends" helps kids feel good—a feeling heightened by the artificial high they experience once they try drugs. No wonder the pull of the peer group is so strong. Once the effect of the drug wears off, however, the need for this artificial high recycles until kids become addicted to the drug itself—perhaps now more powerful than their "addiction" to the group. Kids like this have lost a sense of control over their lives.

They let things happen to them. They cannot, or do not, think of the consequences of what they're doing. Some do not care.

How can we prevent the situation from reaching this point?

The answer isn't to *explain* to children why drugs are dangerous—they already know this. For example, I once asked several eight- and nine-year-olds what they thought about drugs. Here's what they said:

- Drugs are bad for you. You could get diseases and die.
- It's bad for your health. One hundred percent of those people die. It makes you do all sorts of things you're not supposed to do. It might even make you do dangerous things, like even kill someone. People who sell drugs are even more bad. They're the ones that are making people die.
- You can run into a wall and get brain-damaged.

When I asked the same kids what they would do or say if asked to try drugs when they get older, they said:

- I will say, "no." I could die from it.
- I'll just say, "I don't do that." Then I'll walk away. If they follow me, I'll get in my car and zoom away.
- I just won't be their friend anymore. You should think first, think about the future.
- I would say, "Maybe I don't want to hang around with you losers."

Kids are pretty savvy when it comes to understanding the dangers of drugs. They are also well aware of the dangers of cigarette smoking and drinking. In fact, many teenagers have told me that they do their homework in health class while teachers drone on and on about why they shouldn't drink or smoke. One ninth-grader even went so far as to suggest to a newspaper reporter, "They should get the kids into small groups and let us talk and listen to each other."

But for this idea to work, children need to have the requisite skills to really listen to each other, think through the situation, and compose a sequenced plan. Neither the Suggesting Approach nor the Explaining Approach can take the place of critical thinking. ICPS gives children those skills, and the confidence to make good choices. It also gives them an inner strength so they won't need an artificial high, and will be able to walk away from peer pressure.

When I asked Donna to create a story with *sequenced plans* detailing how she would solve the problem of being pressured by her friends to smoke cigarettes, here's what she said:

> A girl named Amy was in the fifth grade. At the end of the year her friend asked her, "Hey, Amy, we're all going out for a smoke after school, would you like to come? You don't have to answer, just be there." They waited and waited for Amy that day. When they didn't see her, they were wondering if something happened to her. Her friend Paula called her that day and said, "Why didn't you come after school to have a cigarette with us?" Amy said, "I don't have to be bothered with things like that. I have better things to do in my life than get lung cancer from cigarettes." Paula said, "Oh Amy, don't be so silly. Just smoke one a day or two a day. It doesn't matter." Amy said, "It does matter, oh it does." Teasing her now, Paula said, "Amy, you won't be cool if you don't smoke," and Amy said, "I don't have to do that to make me look cool." She told her friends she was going to Mr. Spotts, the principal, to let him know that the girls were smoking on school grounds. The next day Amy came to her friends with Mr. Spotts and he said, "You're all sus-

pended from school." When their parents found out, they took them for a checkup and the doctor told them all they had lung cancer from smoking. Their parents couldn't believe it. Amy had grief for them but she tried to tell them. Amy found friends that did not smoke and she knew for sure now that she would never smoke so she would never die from smoking.

Before cigarettes, drugs, and alcohol enter into your child's life, here are some things you can do:

- Help your child actively gather information on the Internet or in the library about the effects and dangers of drugs, alcohol, and cigarettes.
- Role play with your child a situation like being offered a cigarette, marijuana, or alcohol at a party. Let her think of ways to refuse any temptation to indulge in these activities.
- Help your child understand the difference between a social drink by someone of legal age and unsafe indulgence.
- Help your child imagine how it might feel to get high on drugs, smoke a pack of cigarettes, or drink too much alcohol.

You can also ask your child to think about what might happen if he does these things. If he says something like, "I'll feel good," then ask him to think of different ways to "feel good."

When I was younger, thinking of my own way worked for me. None of the scare tactics and *explanations* offered by all my family and friends convinced me to stop smoking cigarettes. I had to decide on my own to quit, and in my own way. Once the decision became mine, I began chewing on oranges. How much more refreshing was that squirt of juice from the orange than the taste of smoke, I'd think to myself. I have not had a cigarette since 7:30 P.M., May 14, 1984—because *I* was the one who decided to quit.

Unsafe Sex and Teen Pregnancy

Teenagers know how to prevent pregnancy as well as they know the dangers of smoking, using drugs, or drinking. Several studies have found that among sexually active adolescents, those who do not use contraceptives seem to know as much about the pill, condoms, and withdrawal as those who do use these methods of safer sex. Even after pregnancy, most young girls participating in these studies knew where to obtain contraceptives and how effective they could have been. Yet the rate of teen pregnancy has not decreased despite this knowledge and the fact that contraceptives are widely available. Instead, it has increased by 27 percent among younger teens in the last few years. Equally disconcerting is the finding that even girls who receive intensive family-planning education after giving birth get pregnant again two to three years later.

In one study Eugenie Flaherty and her colleagues found that girls who engaged in unsafe sex, when compared to those who did not engage in sexual activities or who used contraceptives, were less able to plan ahead and believed pregnancy is something that just happens, deficiencies also found by Barbara Steinlauf. The non-contraceptive users explained their pregnancies by saying things like:

- I forgot my pills when I went on a trip
- I used the money I'd put aside for contraceptives for something else

- My diaphragm was in one purse and I took the other by mistake
- I kept putting off putting it in and then it was too late

And, compared to abstainers and sexually active teenagers who did practice safe sex, these girls were also less able to think of alternative solutions and sequenced plans to problems that had nothing to do with pregnancy—problems such as how to make friends or how to entice a reluctant friend to go to a movie. If these girls could not make plans and think of solutions for the everyday problems in their lives, they would be equally unprepared to cope with problems of this magnitude.

Although the non-contraceptors were able to think of consequences—they knew they'd probably get pregnant—they could not, or would not, think of what else to do. That deficiency, plus a lack of control over what *could* happen to them, no doubt contributed greatly to what *did* happen to them.

Few of the discussions about teen pregnancy ask, "Why do girls get pregnant in the first place?" But this is an important question. Teens and even some preteens may participate in sexual activity for a variety of reasons. They may want to attract a particular person of the opposite sex, or they may turn to sex for the same reason that others turn to drugs and violence: they can't say no, they need to feel important, to release pent-up anger, or relieve a deeper depression. Some girls use pregnancy as a way to get back at a world they perceive is against them, in the same way that other kids turn to violence.

Good sequential planning skills can help these girls think of their long term goals, how long it will take to reach those goals, and how sexual activities that could result in pregnancy could interfere with attaining those goals.

Thinking about external consequences, such as getting caught for stealing, or, in this case, pregnant from unsafe sex, does not stop many teens from doing these things. Teens who cannot control their actions, or who need instant gratification, do not think about the impact their behavior may have on the rest of their lives. And this is no longer just a girl's problem. In today's world, in which unsafe sex can result in contracting sexually transmitted diseases such as herpes or HIV-AIDS, the ability to wait and think beyond immediate gratification is as critical for boys as it is for girls.

To prepare your child to be able to think clearly about issues involving sexuality that will surface in the coming years, and to encourage not just safe sex but even abstinence, here are some things you can do:

- Listen to what your child already knows about sexual activity, both safe and unsafe.
- Find out what your child already knows about the imperfections of condoms as sexual protection.
- Help your son as well as your daughter learn to think of alternative solutions to unsafe sex in light of potential consequences now, and how the consequences could interfere with his or her plans for the future. Remember, even if children are aware of the potential or likely consequences of pregnancy, they may still take the risk—particularly if they cannot delay gratification, have insecure feelings about themselves, or feel angry at the world.

Teen Violence

Parents don't want their child to be the one who starts fights, teases, or bullies other children. Nor do they want their child to be the victim of a bully. Yet the single most prominent concern of nearly every child who participated in our research was just that—being the victim of the class bully.

Studies indicate that one out of every seven American schoolchildren—almost five million kids—is either a bully or the victim of one. One survey found that almost 60 percent of middle school students reported they had been bothered by at least one bully. John Hoover, who has researched bullies, reports that 10 to 12 percent of kids say their lives in school are miserable, and concludes, "I don't think that's something that kids need to go through."

We have seen how bullying Sarah could be, but there are children whose behavior is much more troubling than hers. They torment their classmates more frequently and with more intensity, and are at far greater risk for carrying out acts of violence that might seriously harm or even kill someone. Although most children who engage in bullying behaviors will not later become violent, many of them will enter adolescence and adulthood with a need to control others—and will not be liked.

The children I worked with, and some fifth-graders participating in a seminar led by Sue Ellen Fried, author of *Bullies and Victims*, told us that the children who are not only rejected by others but also feared are those who:

- Scratch, bite, throw things, hit others
- Threaten to hurt others
- Steal or break things
- Get other kids in trouble
- Make fun of kids' clothes, skin color, weight
- Gossip and spread rumors
- Laugh at, make faces, or tease others
- Cheat at sports, razz the other team
- Talk badly about family members, including those who are dead

- Ignore or reject others who are trying to participate in games or join teams

While boys who are bullies may fight and physically hurt other kids more than girls, Carla Garrity, coauthor of *Bully-Proofing Your School*, tells us that girls rely more on verbal and psychological techniques such as excluding a classmate from a birthday party or starting a hurtful rumor.

Some children, as we saw in Chapter 5, have an amazingly mature understanding of what's really underneath the behavior of a bully. Many of their insights were similar to those given to us by experts:

- Power is the absolute number-one issue with bullies
- Bullies feel important by diminishing the importance of others
- Bullying is an attempt to gain peer status
- Bullies, rejected by peers, seek friends who are also bullies, and who feed on each other by thinking their behavior is "macho"
- Bullies feel no empathy though they may be crying out for help by hurting others

Such behaviors, in combination with the almost inevitable rejection by peers, is a powerful predictor of later, more serious violence. They must be noticed, and nipped in the bud. But how?

I once saw a video of an older boy bullying a younger boy in the playground. Though adult aides were nearby, no one intervened. When asked, the principal simply said, "Boys will be boys." Perhaps in today's climate, teachers and other authority figures are afraid to intervene. Perhaps school districts fear being sued by the parents of the bullying child. Or perhaps educators don't have the expertise to deal with these situations. I believe that they *must* step in—and that *how* they do so is critically important.

One school's administration applied the principle of "zero tolerance"—the idea that even the first offense must be punished by suspension so as to inhibit others from acting out. Accordingly, an eleven-year-old boy who had hit a classmate several times was suspended for two weeks; however, no one asked the boy to talk about what he had done and why. By the time he returned to school, he was angrier than when he left, and took out his anger, predictably, on the boy who he perceived had gotten him in trouble. The situation became so emotionally charged that the boy was eventually transferred out of the school altogether.

But the other extreme—not intervening at all—has potentially serious consequences as well for both victims and bullies. Victims may carry unpleasant memories of school with them for the rest of their lives. They also may become depressed, or even later compensate for their fear of others by becoming bullies themselves.

As for bullies, remember the recent news stories from Jonesboro, Arkansas; Pearl, Mississippi; Paducah, Kentucky; Edinboro, Pennsylvania; Springfield, Oregon; and Littleton, Colorado? School-age boys in these towns were so angry and frustrated about their rejection by family and/or peers that they obtained guns and went on shooting rampages in their schools, killing classmates, teachers, and parents. All of these boys (the youngest, only eleven years old) are reported to have warned authorities that they were going to do something "big"; some even said that they were going to kill. No one listened. No one seemed concerned.

Maybe these boys just needed someone to hear them. Instead, the silence they encountered must have told them, "We don't care what's going on in your head. We don't take you seriously." Or, perhaps, "We don't want to get involved." Perhaps some of these boys were in pain themselves and felt that their own cries for help were being ignored. Hurting others was a way to get the attention that otherwise eluded them.

Not expressing thoughts and feelings at all can have equally devastating consequences. A fifteen-year-old boy in Pennsburg, Pennsylvania, was bullied by a classmate for three years. Unlike the boys mentioned above, this boy kept his pain inside. One day he brought a gun to school and shot and killed the bully in front of his classmates. Had this boy been encouraged to express his thoughts and feelings when he was much younger, and had the adults in his life noticed that something was bothering him, maybe—just maybe—this tragedy could have been averted.

Girls also commit acts of extreme violence. although the incidence is much lower. In Philadelphia, a teenager who was described as desperate for a friend finally thought she found one. When that "friend" teamed up with a peer and not only took her sneakers but continued to torment her, the girl became enraged and killed her. Interviewed by police, those who knew the shooter when she was younger said that she was quiet and withholding about her feelings. I wasn't surprised to learn this. Anyone who holds things in for years is like a pot of water left to boil until the lid pops off.

Sometimes girls who long for friends become victims, not perpetrators of violence. One lonely, isolated fourteen-year-old latched on to a group of girls and tried desperately to please them. They turned on her. The leader led the physical attack, and the others watched passively, not coming to her rescue. Were they too afraid of being attacked or rejected themselves? Did they freeze because they didn't know what to do? Were they thinking at all?

Teenagers don't just decide one day to hurt or kill someone. Their anger and frustration have been building for years, as well as their sense that they don't have control over their lives. Imagine how differently these youngsters might have felt about themselves and their world had they been encouraged to think about their own and others' feelings, and to solve problems important to them when they were much younger.

This is where the Problem-Solving Approach can help. The ICPS method doesn't take power away from kids and control them by demands, threats, and physical punishment; nor does it ignore their pleas for help. Instead, it encourages them to regain the very control, pride, and empathy that makes them happy, responsible, and socially competent human beings. Instead of making children dependent on us to solve their problems, ICPS enables them to learn to make their own decisions and become good problem solvers early in life. ICPS children have the emotional strength and ability to handle frustrating moments, and know what to do to overcome them.

Before bullying behavior or being the victim of a bully turns into more serious violence and/or depression, here are some things you can do at the first warning signs:

If your child is *the bully*, ask:

- How do you think someone feels when you hurt him?
- How do you think that person thinks and feels about you?
- How do you feel about his feeling (hurt, angry, sad)?
- What might happen if you keep hurting people?

Search for empathic consequences, such as, "I might really hurt someone," or "I might feel bad inside," instead of external consequences, such as, "I might get suspended," or, "I might get in trouble." At a keynote address to the National Association of School Psychologists, Daniel Goleman told us about a boy who had killed someone and who said, "If I could feel his pain, I couldn't have done what I did."

If your child is *the victim*, ask:

- How do you feel when someone bullies (teases) you?
- How do you think he might be feeling inside?
- Can you think of why he might have a need to do that?

- What can you do or say when you are bullied by someone?

If, however, children are in real danger, then they need to be told that they should notify the teacher or other authority figures about their situation. They need to be able to distinguish between those problems they can solve themselves by using ICPS, and those situations in which adult intervention is needed to prevent harm.

Some Final Thoughts

Perhaps programs designed to simply tell children about the dangers of drugs, unsafe sex, and violence do not work because children simply don't listen. Or maybe children resent being told what to do.

That is why the problem-solving approach is so important. Whether the problem is drug abuse, teen pregnancy (self-hurt), or violence (hurting others), children must be able to take control of their lives and not let things "just happen." Through ICPS, they will learn to trust their own judgment and develop an inner strength to know when to follow others, and when to chart an independent course. The solutions and plans your child may come up with now may never be actually used; some may ultimately prove ineffective. But the most important thing is that your child learn to problem solve when she is young, practicing on everyday kinds of problems, before big problems with serious consequences intrude on her life.

Thinking children who care about themselves and others will be more successful at making friends, and at making responsible decisions in light of their potential consequences. They will feel pride in their successes instead of frustration in their failures. They will have less need to succumb to the pressures of doing what they don't want to do from "friends" they don't want to have.

Perhaps the sixth-grader I mentioned in Chapter 10 said it best: "We have to learn to think for ourselves. People won't always be around to help us."

Let me know how ICPS is working in your family. You can write to me at:

> MCP Hahnemann University
> 245 N. 15th Street, MS626
> Philadelphia, PA 19102

Or E-mail me at: mshure@drexel.edu. I'd love to hear from you.

References

BOOKS BY MYRNA B. SHURE

For Families:

Raising a Thinking Child: Help Your Young Child to Resolve Everyday Conflicts and Get Along with Others. New York: Henry Holt, 1994. Paperback, Pocketbooks, 1996.

Raising a Thinking Child Workbook. Champaign, Ill.: Research Press, 2000.

For Schools:

I Can Problem Solve (ICPS): An Interpersonal Cognitive Problem Solving Program [preschool]. Champaign, Ill.: Research Press, 2000.

I Can Problem Solve (ICPS): An Interpersonal Cognitive Problem Solving Program [kindergarten/primary grades]. Champaign, Ill.: Research Press, 1992.

I Can Problem Solve (ICPS): An Interpersonal Cognitive Problem Solving Program [intermediate elementary grades]. Champaign, Ill.: Research Press, 1992.

BOOKS AND PERIODICALS

Introduction

Aberson, B. "An Intervention for Improving Executive Functioning and Social/Emotional Adjustment of ADHD Children: Three Single Case

Design Studies." Doctoral dissertation, Miami, Florida, Miami Institute of Psychology, 1996.

Bell, R., and D. Pearl. "Psychosocial Change in Risk Groups: Implications for Early Identification." *Prevention in Human Services*, 1 (1982), 46–59. (Reporting research by G. M. Smith and C. P. Fogg, "Psychological Antecedents of Teen-Age Drug Use.")

Dubow, E. G., and J. Tisak. "The Relation Between Stressful Life Events and Adjustment in Elementary School Children: The Role of Social Support and Social Problem Solving Skills." *Child Development 60* (1989): 1412–23.

Elias, M. J., M. Gara, M. Ubriaco, P. A. Rothman, J. F. Clabby, and T. Schuyler. "Impact of a Preventive Social Problem Solving Intervention on Children's Coping with Middle-School Stressors." *American Journal of Community Psychology 14* (1986): 259–76.

Eron, L. D., and R. Huesmann. "The Relation of Prosocial Behavior to the Development of Aggression and Psychopathology." *Aggressive Behavior 10* (1984): 201–11.

Goleman, D. *Emotional Intelligence*. New York: Bantam Books, 1995.

Greene, R. W. *The Explosive Child*. New York: HarperCollins, 1998.

Katz, L. G., L. Kramer, and J. Gottman. "Conflict and Emotions in Marital, Sibling, and Peer Relationships." In *Conflict in Child and Adolescent Development*, edited by C. U. Shantz and W. W. Hartup. Cambridge, Mass.: Cambridge University Press, 1992, pp. 122–49.

Lee, M., P. G. Zimbardo, and M. Bertholf. "Shy Murderers." *Psychology Today*, November 1977.

Morison, P., and A. S. Masten. "Peer Reputation in Middle Childhood as a Predictor of Adaptation in Adolescence: A Seven-Year Follow-up." *Child Development 62* (1991): 991–1007.

Parker, J. G., and S. R. Asher. "Peer Relations and Later Personal Adjustment: Are Low-accepted Children at Risk?" *Psychological Bulletin 102* (1987): 357–89.

PRIDE Survey, in *The Philadelphia Inquirer*, "More Teenagers Using Drugs," Sept. 26, 1996.

Rubin, K. H., and R. S. L. Mills. "The Many Faces of Social Isolation in Childhood." *Journal of Consulting and Clinical Psychology 56* (1988): 916–24.

Chapter 1

Asendorpf, J. "Shyness in Middle and Late Childhood." In *Shyness: Perspectives on Research and Treatment,* edited by W. H. Jones, J. M. Cheek, and S. R. Briggs. New York: Plenum Press, 1986.

Asher, S. R. "Recent Advances in the Study of Peer Rejection." In *Peer Rejection in Childhood,* edited by S. R. Asher and J. D. Coie. New York: Cambridge University Press, 1990, pp. 3–14.

Asher, S. R., J. T. Parkhurst, S. Hymel, and G. A. Williams. "Peer Rejection and Loneliness in Childhood." In *Peer Rejection in Childhood,* edited by S. R. Asher and J. D. Coie. New York: Cambridge University Press, 1990, pp. 253–73.

Coie, J. D., K. A. Dodge, and H. Coppotelli. "Dimensions and Types of Social Status: A Cross-Age Perspective." *Developmental Psychology 18* (1982): 557–70.

Coie, J. D., K. A. Dodge, and J. B. Kupersmidt. "Peer Group Behavior and Social Status." In *Peer Rejection in Childhood,* edited by S. R. Asher and J. D. Coie. New York: Cambridge University Press, 1990, pp. 17–59.

Fried, S., and P. Fried. *Bullies & Victims: Helping Your Child Through the Schoolyard Battlefield.* New York: M. Evans, 1996.

Garrity, C., K. Jens, W. Porter, N. Sager, and C. Short-Camilli. *Bully-Proofing Your School.* Longmont, Colo.: Sopris West, 1996.

Spivack, G., and M. Levine. "Self Regulation in Acting Out and Normal Adolescents." Report M-4531. Washington, D.C.: National Institutes of Health, 1963.

Chapter 2

Batsche, G., and B. Moore. "Bullying." In *Helping Children Grow Up in the 90's: A Resource Book for Parents and Teachers.* Bethesda, Md.: National Association of School Psychologists, 1992, pp. 189–93.

Barber, B. K. "Parental Psychological Control: Revisiting a Neglected Construct." *Child Development 67* (1996): 3296–319.

Gordon, T. *Parent Effectiveness Training (P.E.T.).* New York: Plume, 1975.

Straus, M. A. "Discipline and Deviance: Physical Punishment of Children and Violence and Other Crime in Adulthood." *Social Problems 38* (1991): 133–52.

Chapter 3

Pollack, W. *Real Boys: Rescuing Our Sons from the Myths of Boyhood.* New York: Owl Books, 1999.

Chapter 5

Dodge, K. A., and E. Feldman. "Issues in Social Cognition and Sociometric Status." In *Peer Rejection in Childhood*, edited by S. R. Asher and J. D. Coie. New York: Cambridge University Press, 1990, pp. 119–55.
Goldenthal, P. *Beyond Sibling Rivalry.* New York: Holt, 1998.
Greene, R. W. *The Explosive Child.* New York: HarperCollins, 1998.
Spivack, G., and M. B. Shure. "The Cognition of Social Adjustment." In *Advances in Clinical Child Psychology*, Vol. 5, edited by B. B. Lahey and A. E. Kazdin. New York: Plenum Press, pp. 323–72.

Chapter 6

Shure, M. B. "Interpersonal Problem Solving: A Cog in the Wheel of Social Cognition." *Social Cognitive Development in Context.* New York: Guilford Press, 1982, pp. 133–66.
Spivack, G., and M. B. Shure. "The Cognition of Social Adjustment." In *Advances in Clinical Child Psychology*, Vol. 5, edited by B. B. Lahey and A. E. Kazdin. New York: Plenum Press, 1982, pp. 323–72.

Chapter 7

Shure, M. B. "Interpersonal Problem Solving: A Cog in the Wheel of Social Cognition." *Social Cognitive Development in Context.* New York: Guilford Press, 1982, pp. 133–66.
Spivack, G., and M. B. Shure. "The Cognition of Social Adjustment." In *Advances in Clinical Child Psychology*, Vol. 5, edited by B. B. Lahey and A. E. Kazdin. New York: Plenum Press, 1982, pp. 323–72.

Chapter 8

McCombs, B. L. (as reported in *Parent's Magazine*), "Thinking Ahead," by Roberta Israeloff, November 1995, pp. 126–28.
Shure, M. B. "Interpersonal Problem Solving: A Cog in the Wheel of Social Cognition." *Social Cognitive Development in Context.* New York: Guilford Press, 1982, pp. 133–66.

Spivack, G., and M. Levine. "Self Regulation in Acting Out and Normal Adolescents." Report M-4531. Washington, D.C.: National Institutes of Health, 1963.

Spivack, G., and M. B. Shure. "The Cognition of Social Adjustment." In *Advances in Clinical Child Psychology*, Vol. 5, edited by B. B. Lahey and A. E. Kazdin. New York: Plenum Press, 1982, pp. 323–72.

Chapter 10

Aberson, B. "An Intervention for Improving Executive Functioning and Social/Emotional Adjustment of ADHD Children: Three Single Case Design Studies." Doctoral dissertation, Miami, Florida, Miami Institute of Psychology, 1996.

Witkin, G. *KidStress*. New York: Viking, 1999.

Epilogue

Flaherty, E. W., J. Marecek, K. Olsen, and G. Wilcove. "Preventing Adolescent Pregnancy: An Interpersonal Problem-Solving Approach." *Prevention in Human Services 2* (1983): 49–64.

Fried, S., and P. Fried. *Bullies & Victims: Helping Your Child Through the Schoolyard Battlefield*. New York: M. Evans, 1996.

Garrity, C., K. Jens, W. Porter, N. Sager, and C. Short-Camilli. *Bully-Proofing Your School*. Longmont, Colo.: Sopris West, 1996.

Hoover, J. H. Quote from "Bullies Beware," in *Education Week* (Research Section), Washington, D.C.: May 28, 1997.

Shure, M. B. "Anti-Drug Slogans Don't Teach Our Children to Think." *Chicago Tribune*, November 10, 1996.

Shure, M. B. "Interpersonal Problem Solving and Prevention." Final Report, National Institute of Mental Health, Grant #R01 MH40801, Washington, D.C.: 1993.

Steinlauf, B. "Problem Solving Skills, Locus of Control, and the Contraceptive Effectiveness of Young Women." *Child Development 50* (1979): 268–71.

U.S. Department of Education. *Early Warning, Timely Response: A Guide to Safe Schools*. Washington, D.C.: 1998, pp. 6–11.

Index